The Jersey Shore Uncovered

Beach volleyball, Point Pleasant Beach

The Jersey Shore Uncovered

A Revealing Season on the Beach

PETER GENOVESE

RUTGERS UNIVERSITY PRESS   New Brunswick, New Jersey

LIBRARY OF CONGRESS CATALOGING-IN-PUBLICATION DATA

Genovese, Peter, 1952–

    The Jersey shore uncovered : a revealing season on the beach / Peter Gonovese.

      p.   cm.

    ISBN 0-8135-3155-5 (alk. paper)

    1. Atlantic Coast (N.J.)—Description and travel—Anectodes.   2. Atlantic Coast (N.J.)—Social life and customs—Anecdotes.   3. Beaches—New Jersey—Atlantic Coast—Anecdotes.   4. Summer—New Jersey—Atlantic Coast—Anecdotes. 5. New Jersey—Description and travel—Anecdotes.   6. New Jersey—Social life and customs—Anecdotes.   I. Title.

F142.J4G465   2003

917.49'0946—dc21

                                     2003000309

British Cataloguing-in-Publication information is available from the British Library.

The publication program of Rutgers University Press is supported by the Board of Governors of Rutgers, The State University of New Jersey.

Manufactured in China

To Nicole Gonzalez
Right at the beginning, you were there.

Keeping
an eye out.
Wildwood

Contents

The Jersey Shore Uncovered

A Season Pass

This book is an account of one season at the Jersey Shore—people, places, events, happenings, and encounters along the 127-mile stretch from Sandy Hook to Cape May.

The obvious Jersey Shore subjects, including beaches and boardwalks, life-guards and lighthouses, fishing and food, are covered here. But there are unlikely destinations—an Atlantic City bail bondsman, the nation's longest-running all-women lifeguard competition, an Airstream-only trailer park, and, in a cacopho-nous category all her own, Little Miss Chaos. Never had the pleasure of meeting Little Miss Chaos? You will, in these pages, and remember to cover your ears.

You'll come along on a patrol across Barnegat Bay with the marine police; pay a visit to a Point Pleasant Beach house where the music of Frank Sinatra plays nearly

Route 9,
Bass River

Boardwalk
stand, Wildwood

24/7; listen to participants at the grueling Around-the-Island Swim describe their battles with tides, exhaustion, and face-stinging jellyfish; and enjoy a front-row seat at a bikini contest. Birders, tiki hut builders, seashell salesmen, sandcastle builders, surfers, beach cleaners, wheel-of-chance operators, custard stand owners, banner pilots, Lucy the Elephant, Old Barney, clowns, babies—they're all in here.

We'll unlock the ocean, play miniature golf, spend one weekend in Wildwood and another on an undeveloped island in the middle of Barnegat Bay, consider the

Bikini
fashion show,
Point Pleasant
Beach

error of our ways at the Boardwalk Chapel, find out how Sister Jean manages to feed six hundred people every day, and learn why residents of Ocean Grove write their names on their flowerpots.

So get settled in your beach chair, put on some suntan lotion, and enjoy.

Keeping the beach clean, Ocean Grove

Unlocking the Ocean

Sunday, Memorial Day weekend. The Monmouth service plaza on the Garden State Parkway, just north of Exit 98, is mobbed, despite temperatures in the 60s and threatening skies. Summer on the Jersey Shore is under way, and even Mother Nature has to step aside or risk being swept up in the surging tourist tide. A flotilla of Atlantic City–bound buses—First Priority Tours, T&S Tours, Academy, Coach USA—storms southbound. Their passengers are bound for Trump Plaza, Harrah's, Caesar's, the Sands, and other casinos. Few, if any, will witness the odd little ceremony that will unfold at noon in front of the Tropicana.

On the beach are a distinguished gent in black tuxedo and top hat and a trident-wielding figure in flowing white beard and orange tunic—ancient King Neptune. His thoroughly modern jeans poke from the bottom of his costume's frilly edges. A small crowd gathers; a mother wraps her arms around her eight-

Lifesaver Rick's boat, Atlantic City

4

year-old daughter, who is wearing a blue polka-dot bathing suit. It is overcast, but much warmer than it was an hour north at the Parkway service plaza. "Hello there," the man in the top hat greets a group of children. "When are you guys getting out of school? Pretty soon?"

Not soon enough, the kids are thinking.

A young woman in a bright red one-piece saunters toward the surf; she is Carol Escobar, Miss Atlantic City 2002, and she is accompanied by Mayor Lorenzo Langford.

Someone asks the trident-wielding character who he is supposed to be.

"You can call me Mr. Ocean," says Joseph Polillo, a member of the Boardwalk Living Theater.

"I'm the Father of Atlantic City," announces the guy in the top hat. He is portraying Jonathan Pitney, a doctor who in the 1850s was the first to sing the praises of Atlantic City, whose calming breezes, soothing surf, and healthful recreational possibilities were guaranteed to cure a thousand maladies. With Richard Osborne, a Philadelphia civil engineer credited with naming the streets along the beachfront, Pitney introduced the world to Atlantic City, which wasn't much to look at then.

George slept, or stood, here.
Atlantic City

Trumpeting his cause.
Atlantic City

"When I first came here, there was fifteen- to twenty-foot-high grass and snakes," actor Michael Doyle, in the role of Pitney, explains. "There were only seventy-eight families living on the entire island. This was complete wilderness."

The Camden and Atlantic Railroad first brought visitors in 1854. A mile-long boardwalk was dedicated on June 16, 1870. The 625-foot-long Applegate's Pier opened in 1884, followed two years later by the Iron Pier, which in 1898 became the world-famous Heinz Pier. "America's favorite playground" was open for business.

Sometime around World War I, the city started holding a season-opening ceremony over the Memorial Day weekend. It is called "the unlocking of the ocean,"

Carrying the torch,
Atlantic City

and it sounds corny, but no summer at the Jersey Shore can really begin without Miss Atlantic City striding to the surf and dipping her five-foot-long ceremonial wooden key in the water.

On this particular day, the raven-haired Escobar does her duty, then hands the key to the mayor. King Neptune, seaweed clinging to his fishnet covering, waves his trident. A two-man crew from the Atlantic City Beach Patrol, the oldest paid beach patrol in the world, rows into the roiling surf; one of the lifeguards tosses a wreath on the water.

The handful of spectators cheer. Back on the world's most famous boardwalk, seven-year-old Larry Norflus presides over his lemonade stand in front of the Seashore Club condominiums, which his grandparents own.

"Give it up for the lemonade," Larry tells passersby. "Joggers, runners, walkers, bikers, come and get your lemonade."

" 'Give it up?' " his mother, Karina Perlman, muses. "He's only seven, and he's got the MTV lingo down."

The sun starts to peek through the fog and mist. Traffic on the boardwalk picks up. Another summer on the Jersey Shore has begun.

Battle of the Seafood Festivals

The New Jersey Seafood Festival and the New Jersey *Fresh* Seafood Festival are both held the same weekend in early June. Confused? Don't be. The New Jersey Seafood Festival is held in Belmar, the New Jersey Fresh Seafood Festival in Atlantic City. The former looks like the seafood version of a frat party, while the latter is more family-oriented—bands play on a picnic area in Gardner's Basin, giant inflatable cats are tethered to the stage, and kids can wander through the nearby Ocean Life Center. You can't get a beer at the New Jersey Seafood Festival, although it does feature a wine tent.

If you want to do nothing but gorge yourself to the gills with good seafood, head to the New Jersey Seafood Festival. Pick up clams on the half shell, oysters, fried calamari, and crabcake sandwiches from Jack Baker's Seafood Shanty, Ike's Famous Crabcakes, Matisse, Danny's Steak and Seafood Grill, and other vendors. Shrimp on a stick, teriyaki shrimp, shrimp kabob—it's all there.

The seafood festival circuit is tough. Belmar

One artery-clogging yet irresistible treat—a bucket of malt vinegar-drenched butterfly fries.

On this particular day, the weather is postcard-perfect—hot but not humid, a flawless blue sky—but in this part of Jersey Shore heaven, there is no beer.

For that, you must head south, to Atlantic City.

"Ours is the New Jersey *Fresh* Seafood Festival," festival director Bob Ruffolo says as he weaves through the parking lot in his peppy little golf cart. "The Atlantic City Charter Boat Association started it thirteen years ago as a way to generate positive publicity at a time when there were a lot of reports of red tide, dead dolphins, and medical waste."

Organizers didn't know what to expect of the first New Jersey Fresh Seafood Festival. "There were just five of us [working as staff]," Dara Quattrone recalls. "Ten thousand people showed up. We ran out of food in four, five hours." She smiles. "It was a total success."

At the first fest, food was cooked in a casino kitchen and brought over. Today, the food vendors—thirty-one at this year's festival—do their cooking on site. There are kiddie rides, a petting zoo, live music, even cooking demonstrations. Unlike the New Jersey Seafood Festival, the New Jersey Fresh Seafood Festival charges admission (five dollars for adults; children under twelve free).

"The weather's always been nice," Ruffolo says. "We've had one bad day, but never two in a row."

"Swordfish [cooking] competition behind the Ocean Life Center," a voice crackles over the public address system. A local band plays "Cinnamon Girl" with the appropriate fuzz and feedback.

Guillermo Veloso, executive chef,
Cuba Libre, Philadelphia

At an amphitheater behind the Ocean Life Center, Nicole Martinelli and three other Stockton College students whip up shrimp and scallops in a spicy sauce as a prelude to demonstrations by professional cooks. The Stockton students are winners in a student food competition held earlier. Martinelli is leaving tomorrow for a job at a B&B on the Maine coast.

"I know I just want to cook," the second-year culinary arts student says. "I definitely want to open my own restaurant."

Guillermo Veloso, executive chef at Cuba Libre in Philadelphia, hands out samples of his savory salmon, marinated in rum and served in a mojo of lime juice,

Helena Morlanes Castano, waitress,
Cool Beans Café, Atlantic City

Steve Cohen,
the King of Corn

mango puree, and orange juice. Veloso majored in archaeology at Rutgers, spent three months in Belize, worked at Port Newark, and "skipped around" in the restaurant business before finding his way to Cuba Libre.

"About an hour's worth of work," he recalls of his typical day at Port Newark, where he would serve as interpreter for Spanish-speaking crews of fishing trawlers. "The rest of the time I was eating on the trawlers—the freshest calamari you could ever imagine," he says, eyes alight.

At a nearby tent, faculty and students from Stockton's marine and environmental studies program point out sea urchins, tautog, blowfish, and other marine life in a 5,000-gallon tank. The festival buys the Stockton program something every year from gate receipts—bigger tanks one year, a video microscope another—and awards scholarships to the culinary arts students.

There's plenty of food to eat, from the likes of Dock's Oyster House, Donna's Place, Fat Jack's BBQ (alligator on a stick), and Ace's Famous Crabcakes, but no trip to the New Jersey Fresh Seafood Festival would be complete without a stop at the King of Corn.

"I come here for the music, the seafood—and the corn," says Lisa Karsko of Brigantine, about to sink her teeth into a glistening ear of corn.

Steve Cohen and his sister, Lori Yahn, share the King of Corn crown. Look for the long lines at their booth, their bright yellow roaster wagon, and the table out front littered with bottles of Old Bay seasoning, Emeril's Essence, Mrs. Dash Seasoning Blend, and Parkay Buttery Spray.

"It's the weather, the people, the place, the product," says Lori, explaining the duo's popularity. They work ten festivals each summer. A dozen years ago, their dad,

Allan, noticed the lines at a corn roaster at a Texas festival. As soon as he returned home he convinced someone to make him a similar rig "so he could indenture us for the rest of our lives," Lori says, laughing.

This is their ninth year at the seafood festival. Why does the King of Corn reign supreme? It's not so much the roaster as the corn itself, from various South Jersey farms. Lori's opinion of the Maryland corn they use at the Ocean City, Maryland, festival they do every year? "Big yucky corn," she grimaces.

Behind her, the twenty racks in the bright yellow roaster revolve 'round and 'round like a Ferris wheel. Karsko takes a bite of corn and shakes her head happily. The line is now twenty-people deep.

"A lot of places, people don't respond to corn," says Lori, surveying the scene. "Here they do."

Selling Seashells by the Seashore

There are no Sallies in the Urban family, which is too bad, because this family really does sell seashells by the seashore. There is a Mercedes—their pet bulldog—but the family does not need a fancy car, or any car, to get to work. Rich and Rose Urban live upstairs from the Discovery Seashell Museum in Ocean City—part store, part museum, all fun.

"FLESH-EATING PIRANHA FROM THE AMAZON!" announces a tag on the fearsome fish.

"HAVE YOUR PICTURE TAKEN WITH JAWS," reads a sign inside the gaping jaws of a prehistoric shark.

African land snails, six-armed starfish, 400-million-year-old trilobites, tarantulas, vampire bats (very much dead, thank you), Venus fly traps, and alligator heads can be found at the Discovery Seashell Museum, along with 10,000 species of shells from around the world. Golden couries and tritons from the Philippines. Pismo clams from Baja. Turbo shells from the West Indies. Giant sugar stars from the North Atlantic. Brain coral from Australia; the store, according to Rich Urban, is the largest supplier of coral on the East Coast.

"You're going to find stuff here you won't find anywhere else," says the twenty-three-year-old proprietor.

He and his grandfather, Paul Krish, bought the museum several years ago. The previous owners were strange—literally. Carol and Larry Strange opened the Discovery Seashell Museum in 1969. They called their collection of shells the largest in the world; the Stranges also operated a store in Sanibel, Florida, where they now live. Their kids knew about shells at an early age; Mom and Dad once took them out of school because a huge shipment—about nine hundred boxes—had arrived in Customs.

"The inspectors said they wanted our entire staff present," Carol Strange once recalled. "They opened three boxes. The inspector just rolled his eyes and said, 'I've seen enough.'"

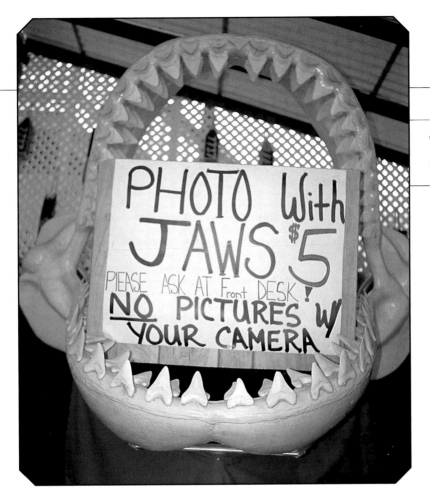

The Discovery Seashell Museum is not just about seashells.

Rich Urban knew about the store at an early age, too. His parents rented a summer house blocks away in Ocean City. He would visit the store "ten times a day, easy." When he was twelve, he started working in the shop. When he was twenty-one, he bought the place.

"The way I look at it, you couldn't have a better job," says Urban, nursing a large cup of takeout coffee.

There are not just shells here, but shells in every possible permutation. Shell angels, shell candles, NFL helmet-colored shells, shell-stuffed bottles, shell-jammed lamps, shell place mats, shell coasters, shell-decorated note cards, shell purses for little girls. You can even buy shell dolls with hot pink shell hats.

Best thing about the store (www.fieldtrip.com/nj): a kid can start his or her own shell collection cheap. A big bag of shells goes for $5.95, two scoops of tiny shells will set you back a buck, or you can pick and choose from the hundred-plus baskets and bushels, filled with angel wings, heart cockles, giant olives, cat's eyes, orange tritons, and other shells. Out back are hermit crabs, described in a handout as "clean, odorless, and very friendly." Low-maintenance, too. The museum's hermit crab checklist: "Changing shell. Sea sponge. Food. Cage. Water. That is all you need to keep them happy."

Sand sculptor,
Ocean City

Adults love the place too, and not just because it's a sure-fire way to keep Jane and Johnny happy on a rainy day. One customer is an interior designer for yachts; she'll stop in and spend two or three hundred dollars a pop on shells or coral.

Where do all the shells come from? Urban depends on overseas suppliers for about half his shells; the rest are collected by friends and relatives. His aunt visited Ecuador and picked up shells; his dad gathered shells in Brazil. On a recent trip to Puerto Rico and the Bahamas, Rich says he picked up "a few shells."

Some shells are not for sale—for example, a Siamese twin helmet shell—two shells in one. "It's a real rarity," Rich explains. "You might not find one if you searched the ends of the earth."

And some shells you couldn't afford unless the Mercedes in your family is a car instead of your pet bulldog. Rich unlocks a display case and shows off the store's most prized possession, a world-record Glory of the Seas cone shell.

"It's huge, it's phenomenal, it's absolutely one of a kind," he says.

And it's yours for just seven thousand dollars.

Boardwalk Chapel

The kinetic, frenetic Wildwood boardwalk would be the last place you'd look for a house of worship. But the Boardwalk Chapel, the only one of its kind in the nation, survives if not thrives in its unlikely spot on New Jersey's noisiest, most uninhibited boardwalk.

"We're not here to raise money, we're not here to show off," says Jon Stevenson, the chapel's plain-speaking director. "Our main goal is to present the Gospel."

He is sitting on a folding chair in the open-air chapel, several hundred feet north of the Wildwoods Convention Center. From here he can scan the arcademanic boardwalk, the ride-packed piers, and Wildwood's famous, free, and impossibly wide beach.

Stevenson, who also teaches social studies at Wildwood High School, has been chapel director since 1977. Len Chanoux served as director from 1963 to 1977.

The Boardwalk Chapel is open to all, day and night.

Game of chance,
Wildwood

"I can't tell you how many thousands of drug users I counseled down here in the sixties," Chanoux says.

One of the chapel's more intriguing features is a "Heaven or Hell Machine," a wooden pinball-like machine just inside the front entrance that would seem more at home in one of the nearby arcades. "Players" answer questions ("All humans are born with a sinful nature"). Answer the question wrong, and a red light appears; answer it right, and you get the green light.

While many of the books and pamphlets inside ("Man is under God's wrath and must pay sin's penalty," says one) do not seem to hold much appeal for the high school- and college-age crowd that has traditionally been Wildwood's lifeblood, the chapel tries not to come off as staid or stuffy.

Car raffles are a Jersey Shore institution. Wildwood

Services, held every night from mid-June through Labor Day, are filled with preaching, hymns, witness, and skits, which can range from puppet shows and pantomime to dramatic monologues and musical numbers (instruments used over the years have included guitars, trombones, and conch shells). There are Bibles in forty different languages, including Amharic, spoken in Ethiopia. The staff—mostly college students—numbers fifteen, and each week there is a different minister.

"This is the one place on the boardwalk that's giving, not taking," Chanoux notes.

The Boardwalk Chapel, a ministry of the Orthodox Presbyterian Church of New Jersey, was founded by the Rev. Leslie Dunn. The first service at what was then called the Gospel Pavilion was held in July 1945. The boardwalk's first head shop, back in the 1960s, was located right next to the Boardwalk Chapel, according to Chanoux.

"Who comes in here now?" Stevenson asks. "Anybody—young, old . . ."

". . . skeptics, believers, the curious," Chanoux adds. "People who want to argue."

"They specifically come in to instigate an argument," Stevenson says.

Most Boardwalk Chapel visitors, of course, are there to attend a service, seek counsel, or find a quiet haven from the hubbub outside.

"Some people just come in to pray," Stevenson says. "I don't bother them. When it looks like they're finished, I go up and greet them." While Stevenson says the main mission "is not to feed and house," the chapel has housed and fed "multitudes" over the years.

Watch the tram car, please. Wildwood

In 2001, the house of God nearly came to a fiery end. A blaze destroyed the building next door; city firefighters doused the Boardwalk Chapel—just forty-four inches separated it from its neighbor—with water, and the seaside church was saved.

"Water was flowing into the chapel like a river," Stevenson recalls. "But I thank God for it. Water," he adds, smiling wryly, "is better than fire."

In a surprise admission, Stevenson says he has been "busted" several times. Well, the chapel anyway, and it had nothing to do with drugs. Just the week before, boardwalk cleaners "ordered" him to pick up litter on the boardwalk in front of the chapel. Nevertheless, Stevenson describes his relationship with the city as "excellent."

Several summers ago, a Boardwalk Chapel volunteer accomplished what might have been a first in Wildwood history: single-handedly stopping the dreaded boardwalk sightseeing train, whose annoying tape-recorded message—"Watch the tram car please"—is familiar to anyone who's been on the Wildwood boardwalk. Seems the chapel worker smacked his head on the wall during a skit. He staggered outside and fainted on the boardwalk—right in the path of the tram car.

"Could you move his leg?" the tram car conductor asked.

"No!" the EMT on the scene replied.

The chapel's future? The Orthodox Presbyterian Church owns the fifty-foot-wide property, which it bought for $2,900 in the 1940s. Good thing; the pizzeria next door pays nearly $30,000 a summer in rent, which the chapel, and its sponsor church, surely could not afford.

The chapel might be more strategically located—it is at the boardwalk's south end, away from the heavy traffic on and around the piers—but Stevenson is happy where he's at.

"Would I love to be where the crowd is thicker?" he asks. "Yes. But this is where God put us. How successful are we? I don't know. We want to present the Gospel of Christ without gimmicks. But we don't want to be boring either."

One visitor told him the chapel would get more people if it dropped four words from its pamphlets and programs: Jesus. God. Hell. Sin.

"That kind of strips the guts of what we do," Stevenson notes. "We might as well sell pizza."

Come On In and Get Some Hot Butt

Wayne Shelton—that would be New Jersey State Trooper Wayne Shelton—stands in a swirl of smoke amid an inferno of fire and brimstone—okay, Patio Chef Natural Lump Charcoal—beer in hand, tongs at the ready.

The air is thick with the unmistakably pungent, husky whiff of barbecue—barbecue pork, chicken, beef. The Philly Pigs are cooking up a storm next door, the Porkitects are just setting up their red-canopied smoker across the way, and two tents down, Dirty Dick and the Legless Wonders, one of the tournament's favorite teams, are up to who knows what.

Shelton, wearing a T-shirt that says "Chicks dig 'um, pigs fear 'um," looks, for all the world, with his moustache and pointy, camo-patterned hat, like Sergeant Slaughter of professional wrestling fame. He proudly points out the technological

Pizza man, Wildwood

Best pizza on the
Wildwood boardwalk?
Maybe Mack's.

Inviting sign, Wildwood

marvels of his new smoker, whose smokestacks,
camo-patterned fenders, and fat tires make it
look more like a military barbecue assault vehicle
than a Fourth of July picnic accessory.

"This is a hobby out of control," the state
trooper says, smiling. "We came here four years
ago, pulled up with two little Weber grills."

You show up at the New Jersey State Barbecue Championship with Weber grills, you risk
serious scorn being heaped on you by Dirty Dick
and the rest of the barbecue bad boys. The state
BBQ contest, held in mid-July, pits teams from as
far as away as North Carolina and Florida against
each other for best-in-brisket, best-in-pork, best-
in-chicken, and, most important, best-in-show
honors.

The Wauhatchie Stump Jumpers won the overall title in 1999 and 2000
(the Porkitects won it in 2001), and teams like Dirty Dick's (runner-up in
2000), the Philly Pigs (third in chicken, 2000; third in pork ribs, 2001), Billy's
Rib Cage, the Big Bad Wolf BBQ Team, and other squads are here hoping to make

Butch Lupinetti, owner of Butch's
Smack Your Lips BBQ

Boardwalk
food, Wildwood

their big barbecue breakthrough. At the very least, it's a chance to show off some cool T-shirts. The Pennsylvania Posse BBQ team's shirts read, "Hey, Sugar, Come On In and Get Some Hot Butt."

The state BBQ championship, held along New Jersey Avenue in North Wildwood, is a fundraiser for the Anglesea Volunteer Fire Company. It's a weekend of good barbecue, beer, and blues; the Anglesea Blues Festival runs concurrently. You can't sample the contestants' barbecue unless you can score an invite to their tent parties or happen to be, say, someone writing a book about the Jersey Shore, but there is plenty of fine eatin' to be had at Ribbens, Papa Woody's BBQ Sandwiches, and other booths ringing the site.

By all means, pay a visit to Butch's Smack Your Lips BBQ; look for the guy with the long whitish beard and a star-spangled Butch's BBQ Sauce cap.

"Lover, looker, barbecue cooker," Butch Lupinetti says by way of introduction. The Mount Laurel resident sells barbecue at twenty-five festivals a year.

"I go on the road in April, come home in September, get about a week off," he says of his nomadic barbecue life. "Barbecue is my business. I can't be a writer any more than you can make a barbecue sauce."

A contestant walks over and asks Butch if his wife has already left to go to

Costco for beef. "She's gone," Butch says. "Damn," the contestant mutters. But Butch, who is not in the competition, pulls out brisket from his fridge and sells it. The man thanks him profusely and leaves.

"Barbecue means different things to different people," Butch explains. "In North Carolina barbecue means pulled pork. In Texas, it's brisket and beef. In California, it could mean tenderloin; I don't know what it means out there."

One tip (learned, unfortunately, from experience): When you see a bottle of hot sauce labeled "Super Pyro" at one of the booths, put it down immediately. Take a bite or two of Super Pyro–doused pork, and a pitcher of beer will not ease the pain. A half an hour later, your mouth will feel like it was blowtorched. Fortunately, the BBQ festival is held in front of Anglesea Volunteer Fire Company headquarters, so medical assistance is just an anguished scream away.

"They're here for the pursuit of prize money [about $10,000 in all] and bragging rights," says Eric Shenkus, the fire department's president.

Serious? The New Jersey State BBQ contest is a Kansas City Barbecue Society–sanctioned event (the society's monthly newsletter is called *The Bullsheet*); judges are flown in from Kansas City. Judging at the BBQ Championship is done on a double-blind system; contestants are assigned a number for each entry, and the number is changed before it reaches the judges. The New Jersey winner gets an automatic invite to the American Royale, a nationwide BBQ competition held in Kansas City in the fall.

Serious? The thirty judges at this year's event outnumber the teams. Judges sit in the fire department's meeting hall—bingo boards dot the back wall—swigging bottled water between bites. "Good, good, good," whispers head judge Ed Roith, polishing off a chunk of filet mignon during the event's "Anything But" (anything but barbecue, that is) competition.

Who enters these contests? The Philly Pigs are mortgage bankers, lawyers, financial planners, and builders. This is their tenth year as a "competitive team," according to pit boss Jim Boggs. In their very first competition, the National Capital Barbecue Contest, they took "a second in sausage." Several years later, they came away with best overall honors. Another year, they placed second in tomato-based sauce at the World Barbecue Championship in Memphis. At the Triangle BBQ Contest in North Carolina, the Pigs finished eighty-fifth out of ninety-five when Boggs, by his own admission, served too-hot ribs.

The Pigs picked up Tabasco as a sponsor two years ago; team expenses for the New Jersey BBQ Championship will run about two thousand dollars, "including

The Cookin' Commandos'
BBQ bivouac

the beer we drink and the fifty times we have to go to Wawa" for supplies, according to Boggs.

Secret to good barbecue? "Time, temperature, and sobriety," he replies. You have to stay sober to do this? "When you wake up at five in the morning drunk and your cooker's cold, you're screwed," he notes.

At the New Jersey BBQ Championship, the teams cook straight through the night for Sunday's judging. Brisket alone takes twelve to fourteen hours at 225 degrees; the Cookin' Commandos use apple, hickory, and red oak. The troopers, all members of Troop A out of Woodbine, do catering and parties. They call themselves "The Special Forces of BBQ."

The Porkitects—architects all—are sponsored by DeGroen, a German beer maker.

"We started out small, with a small grill, and pretty soon said, 'This is stupid,'" Barry Miller says as he cranks up his smoker. Now they work out of a custom-made smoker, with canopy, cabinets, and sink. That plastic countertop? It will be replaced with a stainless steel top next year.

The fifteen members of the Porkitects are charged one hundred dollars in annual dues, which pays for competition fees, meats, dry rubs, and other supplies. The Porkitects won the New Jersey State Barbecue Championship in 2001, but their proudest moment might have been earning two first-place awards in the prestigious Memphis in May competition several years ago. "We did a great chicken," Miller says wistfully.

His team's chances of repeating as New Jersey barbecue champs this year? "Probably slim," the architect replies. "Pretty good is not going to cut it here. You need the judges to say 'Wow.'"

The 3 Ps, from Windsor, Virginia, would get the most wows in 2002, winning the New Jersey BBQ Championship title. It would not be the best of tournaments for the Philly Pigs; they finish twelfth overall. The Porkitects, the defending champs, finish sixth. The Cookin' Commandos—the state troopers—finish seventh overall, up from fifteenth the year before. All the smokers and cookers, lovers and lookers promised they would be back at the festival the following year, hungrier than ever.

"The barbecue bug gets you," Boggs says inside the Philly Pigs tent. "You move up, get a bigger rig. Hopefully you win something."

Lucy

By all accounts, the summer of 2002 was a good one for business down the Shore. Temperatures were off the charts; it was the hottest summer on record since 1895, which meant big crowds on the beach and boardwalk.

The state's only six-story elephant—the only five- or four-story one, for that matter—had a great year. No, make that spectacular.

"Lucy's had a banner year," says Rich Helfant, executive director of the Save Lucy Committee. "Her physical condition has never been better. She's 100 percent restored."

If you're a 120-year-old wooden elephant, getting your toenails painted and your stair treads replaced can make you feel chipper.

Lucy the Elephant is the Jersey Shore's most distinctive—and ditzy—structure. Forget the piers, Ferris wheels, or any of the lighthouses; none matches Lucy in terms of history, charm, and sheer kitsch. She (actually she's a he; more on that later) is unique. It's amazing, considering her perilous perch right on the edge, that she has held up since 1881. What's even more amazing is that most New Jerseyans have never paid her a visit. Helfant can't get over the fact that Lucy is ignored, or at least taken for granted, in her own backyard.

Lucy even gets her toes painted.

An all-American attraction, from an unfamiliar position

"She's a national landmark, but a lot of people in Margate have never been here," says Helfant, a Margate native who now lives in Egg Harbor Township.

"Hi, welcome to Lucy," a tour guide behind him says. "My name is Tyler. There's no smoking or running inside Lucy."

Her history is full of low moments and high drama. She was actually one of three elephants designed by developer James Lafferty. Lucy's purpose was to entice homeowners to buy sandy lots in Margate, then known as South Atlantic City. "My invention consists of a building in the form of an animal, the body of which is floored and divided into rooms," read his patent application. "The legs contain the stairs which lead to the body."

Lucy was built at a cost of $25,000. The other two elephants were the Light of Asia, in what is now South Cape May, and the Elephantine Colossus at Coney Island, a twelve-story structure divided into thirty-one rooms—the Main Hall, the Shoulder Room, Throat Room, and more. The Colossus—billed as "The Eighth Wonder of the World"—caught fire in 1896 and burned to the ground. The Light of Asia, like the Colossus a financial disappointment, was torn down in 1900.

Lucy lived on. In 1902 an English doctor leased it as a summer home. In 1903 a storm left Lucy knee-deep in sand; volunteers dug her out and moved her away from the beach, according to William McMahon, author of *The Story of Lucy the Elephant,* the best concise history. Lucy was turned into a tavern; in 1904 she nearly burned down when a rowdy drinker knocked over an oil lantern. In 1929, a storm tore off her canopied howdah. In 1944, she took another beating in a hurricane. In 1970, Lucy nearly met the wrecking ball; a developer was negotiating to buy the land she stood on. The brand-new Margate Civic Association stepped in, and on June 20, 1970, Lucy was raised with jacks, fastened to I-beams attached to dollies, and towed to her present location in "one of the strangest processions ever witnessed in New Jersey," according to McMahon. In 1971, Lucy was placed on the National Register of Historic Places.

Today, Lucy gets about thirty thousand visitors a year, a number Helfant describes as "insignificant" considering the thirty million-plus who annually visit Atlantic City, a fifteen-minute drive away. Visitors over the years have included everyone from President Woodrow Wilson to Mister Rogers. In the novel *Money Wanders,* by Eric Dezenhall, mobsters use Lucy as their hangout. No one is certain how Lucy got her name, but she's really a he; the Margate elephant has tusks, found only on male Indian elephants.

The only example of zoomorphic architecture left in the country, Lucy depends on seven high school– and college-age tour guides, plus the forty-five members and seven trustees, most of them senior citizens, on the Save Lucy Committee.

"For a lot of the ladies, Lucy is the reason they get up in the morning," Helfant says. The oldest volunteer is Lucetta Israel, ninety-two. "When she works the register, she balances to the penny, every single time," Helfant says. "No one else does."

The gift shop is stocked with Lucy T-shirts, Lucy coffee mugs, and Lucy blankets. The adjacent A-frame building once served as the Camden and Atlantic Railroad depot. While Helfant is happy with Lucy's shape, he is embarrassed by the scrubby grounds.

"This park is a disgrace," the former assistant vice president of entertainment at Resorts says. "It's weeds, dead weeds. It's not befitting a national landmark."

One plan calls for paths and a cascading pool in the shape of Lucy's footprint (for more about Lucy, and updates on her renovation, see ⟨www.lucytheelephant.org⟩).

Richard Helfant, executive director of the Save Lucy Committee

Repairs have often taken on an elephantine pace because funds are often slow to materialize. A $1.5 million restoration project took all of thirty years to complete. "It was a lot of cupcakes and T-shirts," according to Helfant.

Lucy has received the occasional grant, but no tax dollars go toward her upkeep, Helfant proudly notes. Margate does not make any direct donations, but the city, which owns the property, pays Lucy's utility bills. Upkeep is constant; it's not easy being an elephant on the Jersey Shore.

"The last paint job was supposed to last five years," Helfant says. "We didn't even get three years out of it. It wasn't a very good job."

Another contractor—Ashley Painting Company in Ventnor—was hired for the job, and did it well. The paint used on Lucy is a custom blend formulated by MAB Paints; it contains a rubberizing compound that protects Lucy's tin skin from rusting.

"As much as it can, anyway," Helfant says. "In this environment, paper rusts."

But the recent repair work means Lucy is stronger than ever and not going anywhere. "She'll withstand any storm," Helfant maintains. "Next hurricane, you come here."

Now if only more people would visit . . .

"She's all happy, she's all good; there's nothing controversial about her," Helfant says. "She's survived 125 years of bad weather and apathy. She's still here, better than ever. She's an American treasure."

Tiki Murph

Miss Tiki beams, as usual, by the side of the road; Pelican Dave is chain-sawing out back, Pineapple Boy grins from a snapshot on a tiki hut wall, and Black Sabbath's "Paranoid" drums demonically from unseen speakers.

Tiki Murph, king of this sprawling, thatched-hut domain on Route 72 in Barnegat, is troubled, however. Nothing to do with his tiki hut and tiki bar business; it's going strong. Nothing to do with the weather; it's perfect. Nothing to do with Pelican Dave and the rest of Murph's employees; they work hard, and well.

It has to do with the all-important suds supply. Someone has been violating the number-one rule at Tiki Murph's—always replace any beer you take out of the fridge out back. A message scrawled on the battered old appliance, which looks like it predates the dawn of tiki civilization, spells it out: "This Frigidaire works like a bank. You must make a deposit to be able to withdraw."

"Don't have any more St. Pauli Girl," Tiki Murph—no one calls him by his real name, Steve Murphy—grumbles.

A car whisks past on Route 72, horn blaring.

"He's got a million people honking their horns every day," says a twenty-something regular at Tiki Murph's who identifies herself only as Trixie.

"When I first came down here," recalls Murph, a Florida native who opened his roadside tiki business here fourteen years ago, "I had four tikis and a five-pack of beer." The thirty-seven-year-old self-confessed "redneck" smiles. "I couldn't afford a six-pack."

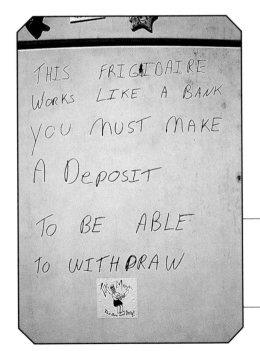

The number-one rule at Tiki Murph's

Tiki Murph
with Miss Tiki

He can afford it now, even if someone is always making withdrawals without making deposits at the beer bank. Murph's is not the only tiki hut business in New Jersey—there's Tiki Tom in the Wildwoods, Custom Built Tikis in Point Pleasant, and Tropical Expressions in Brick, among others—but Murph is undoubtedly the most colorful figure. His can't-miss-it roadside business—look for the tiki huts, thatched roofs, handmade signs, and Miss Tiki, the lei-adorned mannequin at mile marker 13 on Route 72—is a familiar sight for Long Beach Island–bound, or departing, vacationers.

"Your guys' idea of an island and our idea of an island," observes Murph, "is different. In Florida, when you think island, you think palm trees. Up here, it's houses with twelve feet between them."

"Sunny Day. Buy Shades," reads one sign. AC/DC's "Hell's Bells" rumbles from a boom box.

"He usually has Jimmy Buffett playing," confides Gina Smith, who stopped by for a tiki hut last summer and ended up working for Murph. She bought Miss Tiki on eBay and installed her at Tiki Murph's.

Got to have shades
to go with the tiki bar.

Buffett is an appropriate choice; Murph seems to have found his little slice of tropical paradise, minutes from the Garden State Parkway. Instead of Margaritaville, it's St. Pauli Girl–ville; instead of soft sand and picture-perfect sunsets, Murph has his choice of tiki huts under which to conduct business, generally pleasant customers, and the realization that life, and work, don't get much better than this.

"When it's [a weekday] and I'm back there by myself," Murph says of his wood-strewn work area, "it's way cool."

This successful businessman never went to college. Murphy ran a produce market in Bonita Springs, Florida, then was a beer salesman for several years before learning the tiki trade from a guy named "Tiki Jim." Murphy doesn't remember Tiki Jim's last name, as he is not sure of the last names of Pelican Dave, Bob ("the best chain-saw carver around"), and several others who work for him.

Murph says he "didn't start taking things seriously" until several years ago, but from the looks of it—on one summer afternoon he doesn't so much work as hold court—he doesn't take things very seriously now either. A festive, funky, family atmosphere reigns. Darren, his seventeen-year-old son, works here.

Tiki bars for sale at Tiki Murph's

Murph builds tiki bars and tiki huts; he'll even rent you one. The bars and huts are made of Atlantic white cedar. "Cedar lasts and lasts, but it's very expensive," the tiki man explains. "I buy from three or four cedar guys."

Pelican Dave carves the pelicans on display, but Murph carves all the tiki head figures, lined up along the road like statues on Easter Island.

"I carved one for my grandmother that was ugly as [sin]," Murph says, laughing. "She loved it. Still has it, as far as I know."

The regulars include Trixie, who rides a motorcycle, and Pineapple Boy (last name unknown, naturally), who wears a big smile, a pineapple, and nothing else in the photo on the wall of the tiki hut, strategically located next to the beer fridge, that serves as Murph's office.

Most of his customers are cool, but there are those who, apparently not swayed by the laid-back vibe, try to take Tiki Murph for a ride. One guy pulled up in a Corvette and noticed tiki heads marked 40 percent off. He asked Murph if he would take twenty dollars for a head that was on sale for sixty dollars. "You want to give me twenty dollars?" Murph asked. "Yeah," the man replied, sensing an imminent deal. Murph went out back and returned with his chain saw. "What half," said Murph, pointing to the tiki figure, "do you want?" The guy, dumbfounded, walked to his 'vette and drove away.

"With me, it's all about attitude," Murph the philosopher says. "You've got to be a nice person."

He claims to offer "the best bars and best prices." What makes his tiki huts better?

"My leaves stay on," he replied, smiling.

His leaves are cabbage palm leaves, straight from Florida. His tiki bars, with thatched roofs, go for $1,000–$1,800, tiki huts alone for about $800. Tiki figures generally run between $20 and $80. Most of his bar and hut customers are homeowners, although Murph has built or repaired several commercial tiki bars.

"Polynesian tropical is really in," Murph says. "Other businesses are jumping in on this."

Tiki may be tacky, but it's trendy. *The Book of Tiki* and *The Great Tiki Drink Book* were released in recent years, and tiki bars are a fixture at the Jersey Shore. For the latest tiki news, go to *www.tikinews.com*, which features a link to James Teitelbaum's indispensable *Tiki Bar Review* pages, a listing of tiki bars worldwide. Tiki Murph's web site is *www.tikimurph.com*.

Murph's is not strictly a cash or credit card business; he has traded tikis for TVs and VCRs, and not long ago traded a carved bear for a small-airplane ride for him and his son. The Route 72 business is generally open from mid-April to the end of October, when Murph high-tails it back to Florida, where islands are real islands.

Does Tiki Murph open up shop in the Sunshine State? Not a chance.

"You can only deal with the public seven months a year," he said, laughing.

How long will the tiki man stay in business?

"Another fifteen, sixteen, seventeen years," he replies. "I could be bigger, but when people get bigger, they get heart attacks. Happiness is everything."

Pat's Lunch

In a clapboard shack with a million-dollar view of marsh and wetlands, Pat Tirotta serves up world-famous cheesesteaks, soon-to-be-famous she-crab soup, and a healthy dose of South Philly attitude.

"The stuff I make here you can't find anywhere in South Jersey," boasts the eighty-two-year-old owner of Pat's Lunch, just outside Stone Harbor. "I make the best she-crab soup. The best ravioli you've ever had. My cheesesteaks are the best; you'll never get a good one until you try one of mine."

He goes off to tend to the half-dozen soups bubbling away on a battered, pot-cluttered range.

"I don't need every customer," he says, returning to the front counter, which snakes from one end of the hardwood-floored eatery to the other. "I don't make no junk. I challenge anyone to bring in anything better from here to New York. If you don't like what I have, I'll give you your money back."

By turns as cantankerous as a short-order cook and as friendly as a Welcome Wagon representative, the South Philly native (as a kid, he cut rolls at the legendary Pat's Steaks) moved to the Shore after serving in the army during World War II. He says he was in the "first wave" of soldiers who charged onto the beach in Normandy on D-Day.

"Let's go back to 1945," Pat says. "This building was a real estate office. In 1966 it went bankrupt. I bought it. What was I going to do with it?"

A local doctor rented the space for five years. Then came a gift shop. Pat worked in his father-in-law's restaurant—Gerlando's in North Wildwood—before opening Pat's Lunch in the shack on Stone Harbor Boulevard in 1966.

Staff then and now? "You're looking at it," he says. Menu? Look on the wall. Super Cheesesteak. Mile-Long Pizza Steak. Crabmeat on a bun. Lobster on a roll. Homemade ravioli and meatballs. Soups—creamy shrimp, New England clam chowder, seafood combo, others. There are seven faded burgundy-colored chairs at the counter and three tables, sandwiched improbably between lobster pots and

minnow traps. Pat's Lunch is also a bait-and-tackle shop; he can sell only frozen bait because of food-handling regulations.

The shack is listed in Stone Harbor, but it's actually in Middle Township. A red neon "Open" sign glows in the window; a bell atop the screen door tinkles as you walk in.

If there's one item Pat is known for, it's his she-crab soup, which takes "four hours and thirty-five minutes, to the minute" to make. On days he makes the soup, he comes in at three in the morning; other days he's here by five or six. He works until 7:30, eight o'clock at night. Pat's Lunch is open seven days a week, year-round. "If there was an eighth day, I'd be open. My wife, Frances, thinks I'm nuts. Maybe I am nuts, but I like my work. I only need three hours of sleep. When I was in the front lines I never could sleep."

Rule number one at Pat's: You must try the soup before you buy it. No exceptions. He wants to make sure you like it, wants to make sure you don't get home, try a spoonful, and say, "This soup's terrible."

"Try Me—I Gotcha," reads his business card.

And if you sample the soup in the shop and don't like it? "There's the door," he says matter-of-factly.

The soup is not cheap: a cup will set you back $4.50, a bowl $5.00. Pat figures it this way: you buy this soup in a restaurant, it'll cost you that much, and you'll probably get a smaller portion. And what price can you put on charm, anyway?

"I don't worry about business," he says. "I got all I can handle. People come in here, they don't want to wait, they can walk out the front door."

And when will he walk out that door for the last time? The army vet goes to the local Coast Guard station every few months for a free checkup. He developed colon cancer twenty years ago, underwent treatment, and there's been no recurrence. "Doctor says I'm fine," he says. "Cataracts coming on."

Developers are forever knocking on his door. His 100-by-100 lot, with that magnificent view out back, is prime real estate. "I can't tell you what I paid for it; I stole it," he says, smiling. "I got condominium [builders] coming after me. I'm not telling them a price now. When the time comes to retire, I'll know. When I feel I can't operate this place anymore. When I lose my mind."

From the looks of it, that won't happen anytime soon.

Buddha on the Beach

On the morning of the big competition, Katie Lyons walks excitedly to the Eighteenth Avenue beach in Belmar, pails and shovels in hand, feeling not only nutty but confident. The twelve-year-old from Wayne is competing in her eighth straight New Jersey Sandcastle Contest, and this summer she intends to make her big beach breakthrough. How can she possibly stand out among the hundreds of entrants at the sixteenth annual competition?

Several weeks ago, halfway through a bag of lightly salted, it came to her: Mr. Peanut.

At the time, it sounded like a great idea. Judges at sandcastle contests love originality. About the last thing you want to make at a sandcastle contest is a castle, unless you have maidens in distress and burning oil being flung from the parapets. Judges are generally not crazy about fish, flags, and beach scenes—too obvious. Mermaids are fine.

So Katie Lyons walks onto Eighteenth Avenue beach in Belmar on a warm sunny day full of promise and discovers . . .

There's already a Mr. Peanut at the sandcastle contest.

"He didn't unveil it until the last minute," Tim Lyons, Katie's dad, grumbles.

"He" is Bob Cicchone of Bridgewater, creator of the dueling Mr. Peanut.

All's fair in love and the sand-sculpting wars, apparently. The New Jersey Sandcastle Contest will attract a record 431 entries—3,000-plus participants in all—to a stretch of Belmar beach that seems to expand every year. Just three years ago, the contest, the largest competition of its kind in the country, took up the beach from Fifteenth to Eighteenth avenues. This year, it would sprawl from Fifteenth to Twenty-first avenues in ideal sandcastle competition weather—warm with sunny skies and moist, pliable sand, from rain the night before.

There are a few sandcastles on the beach: Castle San Baggio, a turreted castle, and the Disney-Fantasyland castle made by Chuck Feld, one of forty master sand

Katie Lyons of Wayne, builder of Mr. Peanut

Bob Cicchone of Bridgewater, builder of the other Mr. Peanut

One of the few sandcastles at the New Jersey Sandcastle Contest

sculptors in the world. His castle, for demonstration purposes only, isn't entered in the competition.

There are mermaids and manatees; battle and beach scenes; pyramids and patriotic displays; and Jabba the Shrek monkey, which is what Chris Stadler, Dave DiGioia, Rob LaPlaca, and Matt Piano, all of Wall, termed their creation after passersby started calling it everything but what it was—a Buddha, and a rather imposing one at that.

Team Buddha's chances of winning best in show?

"We're a shoo-in," Piano replies. "If there's a best in the world, we'll win it."

Katie Lyons used a flowerpot for Mr. Peanut's hat and a Snapple lid for his trademark monocle. Megan Couchon, eleven, of Freehold Township, who learned of the contest just the day before by reading a banner plane ad, sculpted a manatee, starfish, a "regular fish," and a crab out of the sand. Chris Peterson, Chris Slininger, Mike Loveland, and Bob Cornero re-created the D-Day invasion in Normandy with boats made of milk cartons and duct tape, blood from Kool-Aid, and 100 toy soldiers.

Tina DeGulis and Sara Capuano, both fifteen, from Freehold Township, used red, white, and blue food coloring to good effect on their American eagle. Tina and her mother, Marie, won the competition's Best on Beach award in 1996 with a giant ear of corn. Nicholas Scialabba of Jackson, Tina's cousin, decided to run with the corn motif this year; the eight-year-old's entry, titled "T-Rex Loves Jersey Corn," combined a fairly frightening replica of the dreaded dinosaur and a theme that would do the state Department of Agriculture proud.

And Jeff Jacobsen of East Windsor built the *Titanic*, complete with portholes, smokestacks, propeller, a giant wave, and the unavoidable icebergs.

Sara Capuano and Tina DeGulis, center, used red, white, and blue food coloring to make their American eagle.

The lone seashell atop the ship?

"The pool," Jacobsen explained.

There was a pool on top of the Titanic?

"I think so," the thirty-nine-year-old Jacobsen replies. "I hope so."

Contestants are not exactly angling for fame, fortune, and millions in endorsement money. Best on Beach award is a $200 Earth Glide bike, while lesser winners receive plaques, gift certificates, and other prizes.

Buddha is all-seeing and all-knowing, and so, as it turned out, were his creators. Piano, LaPlaca, Stadler, and DiGioia made good on their pre-competition boast by winning Best on Beach. "Barbie Beach Resort," by Jennifer Kopceuch, Tori Rizzitello, and Dana Kapighian of Belmar, wins first place in the seven-and-under category. A Statue of Liberty made by youngsters from Brookside School earns top honors in the eight-to-eleven category. And Nicole and Mark D'Angelo of Belmar show you can win with a castle in a sandcastle contest with their magnificent "Castle Creek," which takes first place in the sixteen-and-over group. Second place: a mermaid made by a team from Gleny.com of Belmar. Third place? "Ethel the Koi," by Sara Hodl and Greg LaPlaca of West Belmar.

Piano and the rest of Team Buddha complain a little afterward—how are they going to divide up a bike?—and wonder if gift certificates, which go to the second- and third-place finishers, wouldn't have made better prizes.

For competitors, the state sandcastle competition is a lot of fun, but there are sand sculptors out there who take their castles seriously. You can make a living from playing in the sand. Five years ago, Feld, a West Chester, Pennsylvania, resident who started sand sculpting on the beaches of Ocean City, quit his job as vice president of a landscaping firm to become a full-time sandcastle builder/consultant. He appears at competitions worldwide and hosts sandcastle-oriented team-building seminars for corporate clients such as Pepsi and British Airways.

"In June, I was home four days; in September, I will be home two days," Feld says.

A teenage girl walks past Feld's castle and, with awe in her voice, asks, "You won, right?"

"No," Feld replies, smiling. "I'm a professional."

Sister Jean

To get a free meal at Sister Jean's place in Atlantic City, you have to play by the rules.

There are four seatings, starting at noon. Once the tables are filled inside Victory First Presbyterian Church, the overflow crowd is taken to the church auditorium. Don't dare leave until your row is called; Sister Jean, a dynamic woman of sixty-seven who has been slowed but hardly stilled by several heart attacks, will firmly tell you to sit back down.

The rewards for good behavior are substantial, though. It's not only a free meal, it's a good meal, and you can have seconds. You're not asked where you're from or what brought you here.

"I do not call them homeless, I call them guests," says Jean Webster, watching the hungry and indigent file in one morning. "And this is not a soup kitchen. They do not stand in line; we bring them their meals."

Please Do Not Touch Anything on the Table until after Service reads the card at every table.

Five minutes before lunch is to begin, Sister Jean makes an announcement: "Everybody who's got to go to the bathroom go now or forever hold your peace."

If Sister Jean's lunch program appears, to the first-time visitor, like a military operation, it's for good reason. About six hundred people are fed here every weekday, and the rules and regulations keep things running smoothly.

"Why aren't other people in this city doing this?" the founder of Sister Jean's Kitchen asks. "Because people don't have love for other people. People 'ook down on these people. They need to read Matthew 25, they need to change their ways."

Twenty years ago, Webster was a casino sous chef, the first African American sous chef in the city's history. One morning, on the way out the door of her house, she saw a man—"an Italian fellow named John"—rooting around in her garbage.

"You can't do that," she told him.

Jean Webster, who runs her kitchen with a firm but loving hand

"I don't care," the man replied. "I'm hungry."

She took him to Pizza King and bought him a sandwich and soda for five dollars. She told John to come back to her house the next day; she'd feed him. He came by for breakfast, lunch, and dinner.

"The third day, he brought a friend; the fourth day that friend brought a friend," she recalls. "That's how it all started."

Within a year, she was feeding two hundred people daily at her home on Indiana Avenue.

"I was doing it all myself," she recalls. "Cooking and serving and cleaning."

In 1995, she retired from her casino job. The way she sees it, she had no choice.

"I had too many heart attacks," she says. "The doctor said, 'Either you quit this job or you stop feeding the people.' I told him I can't stop feeding the people."

In 1997, the Atlantic City Presbyterian Council offered Sister Jean space and help. She could run her lunch program inside Victory First Presbyterian Church on Pacific Avenue.

And that is where Sister Jean can be found five a.m. every morning, cooking and supervising, making sure her fifteen or so staffers—all but three of them volunteers—are doing what they're supposed to.

"O Lordy," Sister Jean says, slowly getting up from a couch after a short mid-morning break.

She doesn't get around as quickly as before, but pity the fool who gets in her way. For her heart, she takes eight pills when she wakes up, sixteen pills at eleven a.m. and ten more at nine p.m. "I'm a walking drugstore," she notes wryly.

Your problem is that you can't spell.
Atlantic City

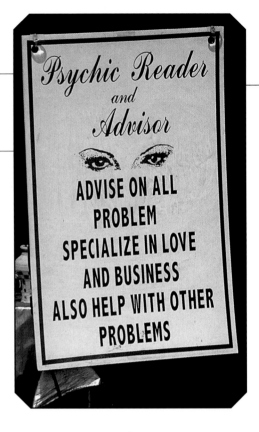

The city sold her current house to her for a dollar; the lunch program's $100,000 annual budget is raised through donations from local congregations, West Jersey Presbytery, the Presbyterian Hunger Project, and fundraisers conducted by the Friends of Jean Webster, a nonprofit organization. About $30,000 worth of food is directly purchased; the rest comes from local bakers, unused entrees from casino restaurants, and private donations. Volunteers are from church groups as far away as Camden and Philadelphia. The Atlantic City Presbyterian Mission Council (ACPMC) pays for her house insurance, medicine, and medical benefits.

"That's all she wants from us," says Rev. Robert Higgs, ACPMC's executive director. "If she got any money, she'd go buy sneakers or steak or lobster for them."

He and Sister Jean estimate that up to half the people who eat lunch here sleep under the boardwalk in the summer (there are about two hundred beds at the Atlantic City Rescue Mission). The area under the boardwalk is known as "the condominium" by its habitués. A half-dozen men and women sleep at Sister Jean's house.

Two of the many volunteers who make the kitchen run

Her head cook is Bruce Agard, who wears a whistle around his neck. "Sometimes you need it," he says knowingly. A man named Willie Ray is her "intermediary cook," while Jack is her doorman. Three of her helpers are known as Big Boy, Big Man, and Big Bubba. This day's lunch alone will require 180 pieces of roast beef, 400 pieces of chicken, and 10 pans of macaroni and cheese, among other items.

"I don't call this a soup kitchen, I call it the house of happiness," Sister Jean says. "You can sit as long as you want. You're happy, then you can leave."

Her daily visitors are a disparate group. Many are down and out, unkempt and unshaven. Some are haggard and red-eyed from all-night carousing or gambling. There are senior citizens from a nearby complex and a handful of young foreign tourists.

"It was supposed to get better when the casinos came, but it got worse," says Sister Jean, who has noticed her numbers increase year after year.

"These are not bad people," she adds. "People deserve a second chance. If they mess up a third time, let them go. I tell people, you're just one paycheck from being in here, too."

At noon, Sister Jean walks to the stage, microphone in hand. "We thank you for the blessings, we thank you for the volunteers, we thank you, Heavenly Father, for always being with us." A short service—those in the audience can stand and give witness—follows.

"I'm home to be with Jesus / Since I laid my burden down," sings Ronnie Gibbs, a local minister. "Burden down, Lord, burden down / Since I laid my burden down / I don't do things like I used to / Since I laid my burden down."

Most of the "guests" join in; some clap their hands. Others, silent, just stare into space.

"He's coming," Gibbs says in his address. "We don't know when He's coming, but He's coming, and He's coming fast. Get ready. This is not 1970 or 1960 or 1950, this is [the twenty-first century]," he continues, his voice rising. "What this means is that you can't be in the crack house if things are going to be all right. You can't be in the doghouse and say this day is going to be all right. It's not going to be all right!"

"The service is not mandatory," Higgs says. "It's not, 'Come to Jesus or we won't feed you.'"

And then it's time for lunch. Volunteers shuttle back and forth between the tables and a buffet line set up outside the church kitchen. At Sister Jean's Kitchen, you can request a "small," "extra small," regular portion, or even vegetarian.

"You got my small?" Sister Jean asks at one point. "I'm waiting. Who got my small?"

Two men sneak in through a side door and sit down at a table. Sister Jean, who doesn't miss a trick, shows them the door. "I love you," one coos at Sister Jean. "Don't sweet-talk me," she replies sternly.

The first shift over, she settles down into a chair for a brief rest.

"Put this in—I need an oven," she says. "We have a stove but it's not big enough. I need a stove where you can put six, seven pots on. Something like that. Put that in."

Greenheads Bite below the Waist

In the tidal marsh of Cape May and Atlantic counties, the nesting season for diamondback terrapins—small, elusive creatures that spend most of their lives in the water—is June and July. The most readily available nesting sites are the embankments of roads.

Oops. It's the height of summer, and the terrapins must share the roads with an endless stream of day-trippers and seasonals, some of whom actually obey the speed limit, most of whom regard anything crawling across the road as a speed bump.

No wonder the coastal roads down here—Stone Harbor Boulevard (Route 657), Avalon Boulevard (Route 601), Sea Isle Boulevard (Route 625), and others—are dotted with terrapin crossing signs.

The other
Shore.
Middle Township

"Each year five hundred or six hundred or seven hundred females get run over," Roger Wood says inside the Wetlands Institute. A chart behind him announces the grim tally: thirty-eight turtles run over on June 1 alone, forty-eight on June 6.

"There's really a lot of slaughter of these reptiles," says Wood, who by and large doesn't blame motorists. Half the roadkills occur at night, when something going about two miles per hour doesn't have much of a chance against something much larger going fifty.

Wood, with the help of Richard Stockton College of New Jersey, students from around the country, and institute volunteers, is trying to save the diamondbacks. Few understand the movements and behavior of this little-known species.

"They're called the cryptic species," says Wood, director of research at the Wetlands Institute. "Basically the only time anybody ever sees them is when females come out to lay their eggs."

He and his students are tracking the turtles' movement with radio and sonic transmitters epoxied to their hard shells. All the terrapins receive three-number codes, so Wood and his charges can determine exactly where they are at any given time.

Five road patrols go out in twenty-four-hour cycles during nesting season to keep the turtles out of harm's way. And all is not lost when a terrapin is run over. Between 1989 and 2000, Wood and his Diamondback Terrapin Conservation Project salvaged more than six thousand potentially viable eggs from roadkilled terrapins. About thirty-five hundred have been hatched; 80 percent of the hatchlings survive and are released back into the salt marshes. Wood and his helpers won't be able to keep the females from crossing the road to get to the other side when they mature, but they are making progress in keeping down a death count that gets little notice along the Jersey Shore.

That terrapins exist in healthy numbers is remarkable considering they were hunted almost to extinction in the late 1800s. Terrapin stew was a much sought-after delicacy; at the time terrapin meat "may have been the most expensive meat in the world," according to Wood.

"There was a terrapin stew fad along the East Coast," he continues. "By the early 1900s, the terrapin population had pretty much been wiped out clean."

But over the years the turtles made a comeback, and today their numbers at the lower end of the Jersey Shore are watched over carefully by Wood and his staff. About fifty thousand people annually visit the Wetlands Institute, an education and research center where you can learn about life in the coastal wetlands, the thin ribbon between land and sea. The cedar-shake, tower-topped building, just down the road from Pat's Lunch, is actually in Middle Township, although most people think of it in Stone Harbor. Ninety percent of visitors pack in between Memorial Day and Labor Day, so if you visit off-season you might have the place almost to yourself.

You don't want to go in the basement. Tuckerton

The private, nonprofit organization was founded in 1969 by Herbert Mills, then president of the World Wildlife Fund. Mills bought 6,000 acres of wetlands, which was then turned over to the state. The institute spreads over 34 of those 6,000 acres, part of the Cape May County Coastal Wetlands Wildlife Management Area.

The institute is a fun place for kids and parents year-round. Programs include marsh safaris, beach explorations, touch tanks, kayaking trips, discovery walks, and turtle talks. The Wednesday night live-animal program is popular. In September, the institute hosts the Wings 'n' Water Festival, a weekend of dune walks, boat cruises, fly-casting seminars, kayaking excursions, food, and music.

The Wetlands Institute is home to the largest colony of laughing gulls in the world. Horseshoe crabs that look like something that crawled out of the muck 100 million years ago. Snails and sea stars, rockweed and rock barnacles, greenheads, deerflies, and a bunch of other neat and nasty marsh bugs. Exhibits inside the Diller Coastal Education Building include the eyebrow-raising "Sex and Gluttony on Delaware Bay." Tanks hold pigfish, lookdowns, and other unusual marine life. You'll learn that horseshoe crabs are not crabs at all; they're more closely related to scorpions and spiders.

You'll definitely want to heed this warning.

Sand Trap
Miniature Golf,
Ship Bottom

Miss Miscellaneous contestants, Ocean City

Hi Lilli, Wildwood Crest

Wacky Golf,
Seaside Heights

Early morning joggers,
Seaside Heights

Oh, you're such a princess!
Ocean City Baby Parade

Evening flag
ceremony,
Sunset Beach

Screaming for joy.
Ocean City

Wildwood

Night, Seaside boardwalk

Surf Tavern, Wildwood

Grass-skirted
beauty,
Ocean City
Baby Parade

Friendship School, Route 9, Upper Township

North Wildwood

Liesje Cardillo, Miss Deckadance finalist.
Atlantic City

Drama Queen.
Clownfest, Seaside Heights

All dressed
up at
Clownfest,
Seaside
Heights

Wildwood

Tara Whalen,

Tee Time,

Ocean City

More

Wildwood neon

Twins-category contestants,

Ocean City Baby Parade

Ocean City

Ocean Grove fishing pier

Lisa Karsko at the King of Corn stand, New Jersey Fresh Seafood Festival, Atlantic City

1956 Chevy
BelAir,
Smithville,
owned by
Charles Lowry
of Galloway

Classic rides, Wildwood

Shady character,
Ocean Grove

Marsh tours last "a half hour to forty-five minutes, depending on the flies and their interest," one volunteer explains. The interest of the audience, not the flies. The flies are always interested.

Did you know deerflies, that bane of Jersey Shore existence, bite above the waist, and greenheads, their equally baleful sisters, bite below the waist? Only female greenheads and deerflies bite—they need the blood to feed their pupae.

"They're taking care of their babies," a volunteer explains.

About two hundred volunteers make the institute work. They staff the Tidepool Museum Shop, make quilts for raffles, and answer greenhead and other questions. Dozens of students in colleges from around the country work here all summer on various projects, including the Diamondback Terrapin Conservation Project, a coastal Ecology Project, and the Pinelands Ecology Project.

When executive director Cindy O'Connor joined the board of trustees in 1981, the institute's operating budget was $50,000; now it is $650,000.

"We have programs every day in the summer," says O'Connor, standing on the outside deck, with its sweeping view of marsh and wetlands.

Multipurpose facility? You bet; you can have your wedding reception on the deck. The observation tower offers "the best wildlife views in Southern Jersey," according to an institute brochure.

For the best quick introduction to the salt marsh, take a walk on the Marsh Trail, which winds for a quarter-mile behind the institute. At high tide, look for grass shrimp and minnows. At low tide, exposed mudflats teem with fiddler crabs and mud snails feeding on detritus. Egrets, herons, and rails try to make a meal out of the crabs and snails.

Most common question from kids here: "What's this?" Second most common question? "Can I eat it?"

So what do you do if you see a terrapin in the middle of the road? Pick it up gently and carry it in the direction it's headed. Terrapins have mild dispositions and are not aggressive. However, if picked up they will flail their strong hind legs wildly in panic; an unprepared person will get scratched on the hands. Don't worry, they won't give you any kind of disease.

And don't try to bring one home for a pet. For one, it's illegal, at least from April 1 to November 1, and the terrapins will almost certainly die in captivity because home aquariums are fresh water and terrapins do not occur naturally in fresh water.

For most visitors to the Jersey Shore, the saltwater marsh is terra incognita; it's something you drive through to get to the beach. Certainly not worth exploring. Stop at the Wetlands Institute and you'll change your mind.

"Most people don't know that when they spread their blanket on the beach they're sitting above 300 kinds of worms and 500 arthropods," Wood says. "There's a whole city of little animals living between the sand grains."

Kohr's

On the crummiest day on the Jersey Shore, when the sun is hiding and the flies are biting and the water is so cold you're afraid to dip even your toes, there's always one thing you can do.

Eat!

The boardwalks almost shimmer in sugar and fat. Hot dogs, curly fries, and onion rings. Pizza, cheesesteaks, and sausage-and-pepper sandwiches. Funnel cakes and cotton candy. Hubcap-sized cinnamon buns and football-sized zeppoles.

The story of the most familiar custard stand on the Jersey Shore starts in Coney Island, New York. The brothers Kohr, who had sold their homemade ice cream to milk delivery customers in the York, Pennsylvania, area, opened an ice cream stand on Coney Island in 1919.

Miriam Kohr and her husband, Mike, own several Kohr's custard stands in Seaside Heights and Point Pleasant.

Can't get any fresher than this.
Seaside Heights

"It was very tiny, a little hole in the wall to be exact," recalls Miriam Kohr, whose father, Elton D. Kohr, was one of the five brothers. "They found they had something people wanted. In those days, we made our own mix—with the eggs, the condensed milk, the heavy cream. It had none of the preservatives you have today."

Miriam leans against the counter of the Kohr's frozen custard stand on the boardwalk in Seaside Park, across from the Sawmill bar. It is one of three Kohr's stands—the others are in Seaside Heights and Point Pleasant—owned by Miriam and her husband, Mike. Their nephew, Greg, owns two other Kohr's in Seaside Heights. Kohr stands in Wildwood and Ocean City are owned by descendants of the four other original Kohr brothers. Miriam and Mike's stands are known as Kohr's; the ones in Cape May County are known as Kohr Bros.

On their first weekend in Coney Island back in 1919, the Kohr brothers sold 18,460 cones at a nickel apiece. Two years later, they opened an ice cream stand in Atlantic City. Then Elton Kohr and his brothers separated.

"We went north, they went south," Miriam says, laughing.

Her father opened ice cream stands in Asbury Park, Seaside Heights, and Point Pleasant. The first one in Seaside, which opened on Dupont Avenue in 1947, still stands. A Kohr's custard machine was in operation at the 1933 World's Fair in St.

Louis. In the forties and fifties, her father made the frozen custard in a giant silver-tubed mixing machine that is still in operation in the Seaside Park Kohr's.

"It's as old as I am," Mike marvels.

A double-amputee, he scoots around the boardwalk in a motorized chair, a Miami Dolphins cap on his head. A sign on the chair reads: "Beep beep, get out of my way."

He remembers the boardwalk in its glory days, in the forties and fifties. "The games of chance were not completely legal," he says, grinning. A kiddie train ran through Steve D's Arcade. The Strand movie theater was just around the corner. It is now a parking lot.

"Seaside had more of a family atmosphere," he recalls. "Now, it's more kids, and they're feeling their oats."

Neither he nor Miriam wants to be anywhere else.

"I love the action, the carnival atmosphere," Miriam says. "Nighttime, when the lights sparkle and the rides go round."

Kate Corcoran,
who works for Miriam
and Mike in Seaside

"Nothing else in the nation has the carnival atmosphere of Wildwood or Seaside," Mike adds.

Legions of high school and college students have worked at Kohr's over the years. Six flavors of soft ice cream and thirteen flavors of hard ice cream are generally available. Most popular flavor in Seaside Park: vanilla. Most popular flavor in Point Pleasant: orange/vanilla twist. You can also get shakes, slush, and Italian ice. It all adds up to instant relief on sweltering summer days and nights.

"Making [custard] is an art," Mike says. "There are no computers, no buttons. It's like when Grandma made the cake. You didn't know what she put into it, what she was doing, but it always came out right. If you don't do this right, you can freeze up the machine. It'll end up in the junkyard."

There are nearly fifty Kohr Bros. stands nationwide—eleven in New Jersey, eight each in Maryland and Virginia, six in Florida, five in Pennsylvania. The Kohr Bros. maintain a web site (*www.kohrbros.com*), with corporate headquarters in Charlottesville, Virginia. Miriam and Mike have no web site, and Miriam's office is above the Seaside Park stand.

"We are little—pennies, nickels, dimes, and quarters," Miriam insists.

She is an unabashed Seaside fan, warts and all. "Seaside will always be Seaside; it will never die," she says. "They're cleaning up the downtown area."

Some Shore visitors, she adds, think Seaside is "beneath" them. "To each his own," she says, smiling. "Some people love vanilla ice cream, some people like chocolate."

Bonding with the Birders

Bazooka-sized scopes slung over their shoulders, binoculars in hand, field guides stuffed in side pockets, a dozen people trudge through a narrow cleft between grass and brush off Sunset Boulevard in Lower Township. It is 7:30 a.m. on a mid-July Monday morning, and it is already sweltering.

"You are here at the only time of day when the temperature can support life," Pete Dunne cracks.

Minutes before, he had completed his customary pre-walk binoculars check, making sure the birders were using the right equipment and using it properly.

"Binoculars are supposed to be used with one hand," Dunne explains, speaking in a low throaty bass. "The other hand is just used for stability."

And now the group, in tight military formation, is ready for action.

Doesn't take long.

Pete Dunne, a vice president of the New Jersey Audubon Society, leads Monday morning bird walks from the Cape May Migratory Bird Refuge.

"Red-winged blackbird," Dunne says, identifying the tiny blur of color and motion streaking overhead.

"Osprey carrying a fish," someone shouts. "Big fish."

"Two skimmers behind us," Dunne says of the long-winged, graceful birds. "Wingbeats don't drop below the horizon." His ears perk up. "A skimmer just called. It's almost a laugh, a guffaw."

Suddenly, the air is alive with sound of beating wings. "Cedar waxwing," Dunne continues. "See if you can see a yellow band on the tip of the tail." His head swivels. "American goldfinch. Nope, a house goldfinch. Same hippity-hoppity."

While at least one member of the group tries to figure out how a bird can be hippity-hoppity, Dunne does rapid-fire aerial IDs. "Greater yellow legs. We have a Forster's tern in front of us. During the summer, the trick is to tell a common tern from a Forster's tern. Yellow warbler going left, overhead. It's a migrating bird. There's no reason for it to be up there unless it wants to be somewhere else. Marsh wren? Sounds like someone is doing a fast rewind on a cassette? That's it. There's an American crow out there. How about that. We usually have fish crows out there. Everybody have their minimum daily allotment of lesser yellow legs?"

It's enough to make the nonbirder dizzy. Dunne, a vice president of the New Jersey Audubon Society and director of the Cape May Bird Observatory, leads Monday morning bird walks June through mid-November. The walks depart from the Nature Conservancy's Cape May Migratory Bird Refuge parking lot on Sunset Boulevard, just outside Cape May, which might be the center of the New Jersey birding universe. During fall migration, more than one hundred thousand birds will flit and fly through the area—every day. "An amazing spectacle," the fifty-year-old Dunne says.

Birders pump big bucks into the New Jersey economy; wild animal enthusiasts—birders, whale watchers, and others—spent $1.24 billion on hotel rooms, food, and equipment in New Jersey in 2001—significantly higher than the $987 million spent by hunters and fishermen. New Jersey is one of only seven states where those watching animals have a bigger economic impact than those trying to catch them have.

One of the biggest birder gatherings is the New Jersey Audubon Society's Cape May Autumn Weekend and Bird Show, which attracts 35,000 birders from around the country. And don't forget the Society-sponsored World Series of Birding in May, a madcap race around New Jersey by birders trying to see who can identify the most species. A record eighty teams entered the 2002 World Series of Birding, won by the Cornell Sap Suckers of Ithaca, who spotted 224 species, 5 fewer than the record.

"For 364 days out of the year, I enjoy watching birds, and one day out of the year, I revert to my childhood and go off on a treasure hunt," says Dunne, who founded the World Series of Birding, originally called the Birdathon, in 1984.

The Cape May Bird Observatory (*www.njaudubon.org/calendar/calCMBO.html*), run by the New Jersey Audubon Society, offers myriad programs throughout the year: Hawk ID Workshop. Back Bay Birding by Boat. Stone Harbor Point Bird Walk. Ghost Crabs: The Good, the Bad, the Ugly. A Butterfly and Dragonfly Walk led by Louise Zemaitis, coordinator of the observatory's Monarch Monitoring Project. There's even a program called Cruisin' for Chicks at Sunset, a three-hour early-evening boat ride past nesting colonies of Forster's terns, laughing gulls, American oystercatchers, clapper rails, and other birds.

No wonder Dunne describes what he does as "a dream job, dream location, dream organization."

Growing up in Morris County, he started birding when he was seven.

"Didn't have a clue what I was doing," he recalls. "Didn't know where the horizon was. Didn't know what I didn't know."

He learned quickly enough. He and a kid from the neighborhood formed their own birding club; Dunne recorded field notes in a journal. In high school, he was more hunter than birder, but an early September day spent at a hawk-watching lookout in Pennsylvania—at one point he was surrounded by a "kettle of raptors"—made him a birder for life. He is the author of several books, including *Tales of a Low-Rent Birder* and *Before the Echo: Essays on Nature*.

Couched in soggy velour, wrapped in resignation and the passenger seat, is
American Birds' Regional Editor Bill Boyle. Visible in the rear view mirror:
Pete Bacinski, the J. J. Audubon of Lyndhurst, New Jersey, and David Sibley, the
hottest thing to hit birding since the Phoenicians melted sand. Beneath us is a
Saab 900 Turbo. Behind us, the 1983 Birdathon.

—Tales of a Low-Rent Birder

Sibley, a former New Jerseyan, is the author of the lavish, definitive *Sibley Guide to Birds*, which the only nonbirding member of Dunne's Monday morning walk found himself buying later in the Cape May Bird Observatory gift shop.

Dunne's group continues on. Overhead are more lesser yellowlegs, slender, elegant wading birds that do indeed have yellow legs and make a repeated "tiw" sound when agitated and a rising, trilled "kleet" when alarmed. Not to be confused with its threat, a low, rolling trill, or its "display song," a rapid, rolling "towidya-wid, towidyawid."

(*The Sibley Guide* did come in handy).

"It chases fish," Dunne says of the yellowlegs. "It picks them up in its bill, swishes them around. It always acts like it's angry."

The birders pause in a marshy area several hundred yards from the beach. "Least bittern," Dunne says suddenly. "It's the Wright Brothers of birds. A weak flyer. You see one up in the air, you go, wow, it actually flies! They spend most of the time skulking in the weeds, frustrating me."

On the beach, a platoon of sanderlings—sandpipers—work the surf's edge. The bird-watchers have positioned their scopes on the sand as if awaiting the next rocket flight at Cape Canaveral. "Petrel," Dunne announces, "flying brrrp brrrp. They look like the least sandpiper on steroids. Purple martin, two broad wings. Shore birds coming across, sandpipers behind."

He takes a moment to plug Peter Matthiesen's *The Wind Birds*, "probably the finest nature-writing ever." And then it's back to the birds without missing a beat. "Pectoral sandpiper," he says, eyes narrowing. "A great big beefy steroid-ridden, Bulgarian weight-lifting program sandpiper, with a sharply truncated corduroy bib."

The only nonbirder in the group is not sure exactly what all that means, but it sure sounds neat.

"That's a common tern calling," Dunne says. "Kee-er, kee-er. Very harsh call."

At 9:30 a.m., the group is back in the parking lot, packing up their scopes and binoculars.

For Dunne, the Monday morning bird walk is job, hobby, therapy, and motivational tool all wrapped up in one.

"I always start the week off this way," he explains. "It helps me keep my sanity. Primes me for the week ahead."

Two Hundred Women Lifeguards, One Writer

Nearly two hundred beautiful, athletic young women in red Speedo one-piece bathing suits and bikinis gather on the beach on a dazzling July morning.

A reporter wanders in and out of the multitudes, shooting more pictures than he has ever shot in one place in his life.

Sometimes you have to take one for the team.

Covering the All-Women Lifeguard Tournament at Sandy Hook actually turned out to be one of the tougher assignments for this book. It's not easy taking pictures and interviewing someone at the same time, especially when all your subjects are wearing bathing suits that don't seem to be as much put on as painted on.

"We don't have beaches like this back home," twenty-two-year-old Emmanuella Ruel says as she scans a stretch of sun-kissed beach at Sandy Hook. Ruel, a lifeguard at a Hilton hotel back home in Quebec, smiles. "Right now, I am not training at all. I could be in much better shape."

We should all be in such horrible shape. Ruel is 1 of 184 contestants at the eighteenth annual All-Women Lifeguard Tournament, the country's oldest and largest women lifeguard competition. Held its first sixteen years at Jacob Riis Park in Rockaway Beach, Queens, and

Stretching out.
All-Women Lifeguard Tournament

And they're off! Lifeguards at the start of a relay event.

Elbows flying, beach flag contestants make a mad dash at the finish.

the past two years at Sandy Hook, the competition is a series of nine challenging if not formidable events, all showcasing essential lifeguard skills such as running, swimming, surf rescue, and surfboat rowing.

Which doesn't quite explain the beach flag contest, a sandy synthesis of musical chairs and WWE grudge match. Competitors first lie facedown in the sand, elbows fully extended. On a signal, they raise and lower their chins, and then jump up and dash 25 yards to grasp one of a row of batons stuck in the sand. The contestant who comes up baton-less each round is eliminated; last woman standing wins. The final few yards is elbowing, sand-spraying pandemonium, as contestants dive headfirst, grapple, and fight for batons, sometimes waiting to let others grasp and miss before making their move. "Sea-gulling," one competitor calls it, a reference to sea gulls hanging back from the pack to snatch overlooked French fries off the boardwalk.

Two Island Beach
State Park lifeguards

The competition, held on a warm, sunny day under a flawless blue sky, draws lifeguards from as far south as Florida and as far north as Nova Scotia and Quebec to the Gateway National Recreation Area at Sandy Hook. Caroline Pierre, Ruel's teammate on the Quebec squad, flew from San Diego to Quebec City, then the two took turns driving in a van to Sandy Hook.

"Prior to this, if women wanted to compete in lifeguard tournaments, they had to compete in separate women's divisions in men's tournaments," explains Brian Feeney, a National Parks Service spokesman.

Forget the "Baywatch" stereotypes. Women lifeguards, at least those in this tournament, are agile, athletic, and competitive. In the run-swim-run event, contestants run 150 yards, swim 350 yards, and run 150 yards. In the ironwoman event, they run 150 yards, swim 250 yards, run 50 yards, paddle about 400 yards, then run another 150 yards to the finish line.

Like any athletic competition, there are the usual pre-race jitters.

"I'm nervous," says Denise De Oliveira of Toms River, a member of the Island Beach State Park Beach Patrol.

What's to be nervous about?

"Not finishing—and drowning," the twenty-year-old replies, smiling.

She finishes, and doesn't drown.

Ask these women why they want to be lifeguards, their first reply is "Best summer job ever."

The Jersey Shore Uncovered

Christine McCabe, a Long Branch lifeguard, exults after winning the beach flag competition.

"Get to spend all day on the beach," says Maureen Klaslo of Toms River, a lifeguard at Island Beach State Park.

"It's great to help people," says Deanna Vogt of Oakhurst, a Long Branch lifeguard.

"Be on the beach," adds Amy McCabe of Eatontown, another Long Branch lifeguard.

"Get a great tan," pipes in sis Christine McCabe.

This morning she's here to compete. Christine McCabe, her fellow guards agree, is the Long Branch squad's best chance of a high finish today. She doesn't let them down. Pushed near the beach flag finish line by a competitor, a rules disqualification,

A lifeguard team pushes their boat to the starting line for a race.

Emmanuella Ruel of Quebec, who won several events at the lifeguard tournament

McCabe wins the Division 2 beach flag championship, giving Long Branch its first-ever title in its first-ever all-women's lifeguard tournament. Squads at the tournament are grouped in divisions depending on the beach patrol's overall female membership—1 to 4 members, Division 1; 5 to 9, Division 2; 10 and above, Division 3.

Maxine Patroni and Debbie Crane, one of five women lifeguards in the sixty-member Margate Beach Patrol, drove up with Maxine's parents, Tony and Patty, to compete in just one event—the surfboat challenge, where lifeguards row a course of about 1,000 yards. They use a boat designed and built by Tony Patroni; the women had rowed it for the first time just the day before.

"Pay attention, girls," Patty Patroni shouts as her daughter, fifteen, and Crane, twenty-four, fight the surf. "Come on, Max. Get going, baby."

Several minutes later, Mom runs excitedly up the beach. "They won! They won!" she shouts.

De Oliveira says she's a lifeguard "lifer"—she's going to stay on the beach as long as she can. She's about to start a career as a teacher, so summers will be open.

"It keeps you in shape; I'm in the best shape of my life," De Oliveira says.

"If you're going to the beach, you might as well get paid for it," says seventeen-year-old Jordan Lorah, a member of the Delaware State Parks Beach Patrol.

Ruel stands ankle-deep in the surf between events, a bemused look on her face. "We don't have seas, we don't have waves," she says. "We have to go far to compete."

By the end of the day, her fellow lifeguards will wish she had gone somewhere else to compete. Ruel starts off by winning the run-paddle-run and run-swim-run events in her division.

"I have to go now," she says. "I want to do well in the irongirl."

The third-year university student wins the ironwoman event as well, crossing the finish line before her nearest competitor, well down the beach, even staggers out of the surf.

All Frank, All the Time

In a house on the Point Pleasant Beach boardwalk that offers a front-row seat to the lively beach volleyball scene, Paul Smith plays his music around the clock, and the neighbors never complain. He loads up his 200-disc changer at eight in the morning and keeps it on all day and all night. Even if Smith goes out for a few hours, the music stays on. It's not big band or Dixieland, Motown or R&B, rock 'n' roll or heavy metal.

It's all Frank, all the time; Ol' Blue Eyes might describe Smith's undying devotion as a pocketful of miracles.

"I was in the music business all my life," the seventy-two-year-old explains. "Frank Sinatra was just the best."

Around here, the home in which Smith and his wife, Anita, live is known simply as "the Sinatra house." Passersby will often sit on one of the boardwalk benches and enjoy the free concert. Some have mistaken the home for a bed-and-breakfast. One guy walked in, sat down at Smith's bar and ordered a Scotch and water.

Smith can't pinpoint exactly when his passion for Sinatra began. Born and raised in St. Louis, his first job was as an appliance store salesman. One day, the owner started stocking Columbia phonographs and long-playing records. Smith became friendly with the Columbia reps when they visited the store; they eventually gave him a job. He worked in St. Louis and Chicago before being transferred to New York in the early 1960s. By the time Smith retired in 1969, Sony had bought Columbia, and Smith had risen to chairman of the company's music distribution division.

He and Anita bought the house in Point Pleasant sixteen years ago, and Smith found the beachfront home a perfect stage for playing the Chairman of the Board's music—and maybe for picking up a few converts along the way. "The house was a shambles when we bought it; we had it rebuilt," recalls Smith, sitting on his patio. "It took a year to rebuild it. As soon as it was rebuilt, we started playing."

Gonna take a sentimental journey,
Gonna put my heart at ease.

Smith owns sixty Sinatra CDs. The singer recorded 2,000 songs and released 100-plus albums. Smith's favorite? Don't ask him to single out one. He prefers the up-tempo tunes like "Come Fly with Me" over the more melancholy numbers like "In the Wee Small Hours."

Smith met Sinatra several times. One night he was having dinner in New York City with colleagues from Columbia Records. Sinatra, with an entourage that included then–vice president Spiro T. Agnew, stopped at the table to chat for fifteen minutes.

Smith has heard all the reports and rumors about his idol—"there have been some terrible stories"—but they haven't dimmed his ardor one bit. "The three or four times I met him he was a gentleman," he says.

Call me irresponsible,
Yes, I'm unreliable.

Each day's Sinatra soundtrack depends on what mood Smith's in. Sometimes he pops in twenty CDs, sometimes forty. Sometimes all sixty go in the changer. Only when he and Anita leave for the weekend does the music stop.

In all these years, only two people have complained. "I don't think they liked anything," Smith says, smiling slightly. "You could have played the Hallelujah Chorus, they wouldn't have liked it." His smile broadens. "I've had a lot of complaints from people when they don't hear it."

COME REST
AWHILE
1923   1996

For some, the music revives long-dormant memories of Ol' Blue Eyes. "Just the other day a woman stopped by and said that as a teenager she stood in front of the Paramount Theater waiting to see him."

The day Frank Sinatra died, Smith taped a half dozen pictures of the singer to his fence. It became a local shrine to the Chairman of the Board. "People actually stopped by and brought me flowers," he says in awe.

> Yes, sir, that's my baby,
> No, sir, don't mean maybe.

"I don't know he had the best voice, but his phrasing was impeccable," Smith says. "There were some other great singers like Tony Bennett, but Frank is just the best."

He doesn't belong to any Sinatra fan clubs; he doesn't feel a need for it. When you can play all Frank all the time on an oceanfront stage, who could ask for anything more?

Note: Paul Smith passed away on New Year's Eve, 2002.

Hot Dog Queen of the Jersey Shore

Celia Maybaum is Hot Dog Queen of the Jersey Shore by official proclamation. You could look it up.

"Now therefore, I, Joan Haberle, Secretary of State of the State of New Jersey, do hereby proclaim Mrs. Max the Hot Dog Queen of the Jersey Shore," reads the 1991 proclamation on the wall of Max's Famous Hot Dogs in Long Branch.

Pictures of everyone from Bruce Springsteen and the late Cardinal John O'Connor to Danny DeVito and Hulk Hogan line the walls of the legendary hot dog stand, which opened on the Long Branch boardwalk in 1928. And Maybaum, known as "Mrs. Max" to generations of devoted fans, is not shy about establishing her place in the annals of hot dog history.

"I guess I'm famous," she says, her hoop earrings dangling. "I'm known the world over. I'm like a president."

Celia Maybaum, the Hot Dog Queen of the Jersey Shore

President, Friend of Assorted Rock Stars and Cardinals, and the Jersey Shore's Official Hot Dog Queen: Celia Maybaum is one of those people who can take over a room, or a hot dog stand, by sheer personality.

"I'm not a little chicken anymore," she says, apologizing for her allegedly slower pace these days.

Apparently, the trip to Denver over the holidays and the excursions to Vegas and Venezuela several years ago don't count. And the cruises to Alaska and the Caribbean.

She is from the Bronx, where she met and married a guy from Brooklyn named Mo Levy. After Mo passed away, she moved to Florida to live with her mother. There, she met her second husband, Milford Maybaum, who had taken over a hot dog stand on the Long Branch boardwalk named Max's after the original owner, Max Altman. Maybaum died in 1980, but Max's Famous Hot Dogs, and Mrs. Max, seem destined to last for a long time.

"The first year we were on the boardwalk there was a fire," she recalls. "Then there was another fire. Then a hurricane."

She opened Max's at its current location, on Ocean Boulevard, fifteen years ago, in the former Surf Club.

"I told Bobby [her son-in-law], 'We'll take [the building] and light it up like Luna Park,'" Maybaum recalls.

Max's is more food emporium than hot dog stand; there is seating for 100-plus patrons, the walls are filled with colorful food signs, and there's beer on tap. Good hot dogs, excellent chili, and you must try Mrs. Max's cheesecake.

Route 35, Neptune

Tending the grill at Max's Famous Hot Dogs

Jennifer Maybaum, Celia's granddaughter

"Everything in it is absolutely delicious," she says. Hey, you don't get to be Hot Dog Queen of the Jersey Shore by being modest.

She swears she is not revealing her age, then relents and says she is "about like eighty," and "kind of like a little retired." Asked if she would ever consider moving Max's from Long Branch, she replies, "Nevah," in an accent that is straight out of the Bronx.

"Max's is a landmark," she explains. "Max's is known the world over. There was once a man who got off a flight from London. The first thing he did was come to Max's."

She says hello to a regular at the front counter, then leans over and whispers, "That's Bruce Springsteen's father-in-law. Patti's father."

Everyone, it seems, has been to the hot dog stand by the sea: Governors and would-be governors, actors and actresses, singers and comedians.

"Jackie Mason was in here last year," Mrs. Max says, her eyes twinkling. "He had people in the back hysterical."

A wrap-around counter offers scenic views over the grill area. Pots of steaming sauerkraut and huge eight-pound jars of Gulden's Spicy Brown Mustard, not to mention napkins, are within easy reach on the counter. The menu includes hot dogs, burgers, grilled tuna sandwiches, steak sandwiches, cheese fries, onion rings, and chicken tenders. When Maybaum started working at Max's in the 1960s, hot dogs were a quarter. A chili dog now costs $3.99.

The Hot Dog Queen gets to work around eleven a.m., helping out where she can.

"I'm just a figurehead here," she says, not displeased by the prospect. "I sit around and say hello to everyone. I'm my own boss. I do what I want."

She's a regular at the Monmouth Park racetrack; asked if she has any other hobbies, she is stumped for a moment.

"I've been so into Max's," she replies. "Thirty-five years of Max. This is all I did, all I knew. This was my life. I've done a lot. It's time for me to take a little rest."

Which doesn't involve having someone else make the chili or cheesecake. That's Mrs. Max's job, one she doesn't intend giving up anytime soon.

"How long will I be here?" she asks. "Until God lets me. Who knows? We have to live from one day to another. Life is beautiful. You have to keep a good attitude on life. Even if you don't, you must."

If she could choose her epitaph, what would it be?

"Mrs. Celia Maybaum," she replies. "Always kept smiling."

Free Diapers for All

The cutest babies anywhere, swaddled in blankets, balloons, and plastic vegetables.

Little girls in grass skirts and oversized sunglasses, frolicking under plastic palm trees. Little boys dressed as surfers, lifeguards, and Ken, even if he's driving Barbie's Jeep.

Kids being towed in everything from coolers and red wagons to miniature diners and floats. An exuberant, joyous, nonstop celebration of kids, kookiness, and kitsch.

On top of that, more twins than you'll ever see in one place at one time.

It can mean only one thing: the Ocean City Baby Parade is rolling down the boardwalk.

"The baby parade is one of the most important events of the season," says Ann Egner, head judge for Division B, the parade's comic category, trying to be heard above the tumult in the Ocean City Sports and Civic Center.

It is a bright sunny Thursday morning in early August, and the hall is wall-to-wall tots, dolled up in costumes that would do a fashion designer proud. There are firefighters and policemen, princesses and angels, bathing beauties and beach bums. Buccaneer Bobby, Little Miss Butterfly, and Cinderella. Bam Bam and Betsy Ross. The Good Ship Lollipop, Noah's Ark, and the "U.S. Kiddie

What's Ken doing driving Barbie's Jeep?

Coast Guard." Kids posing as pizza, tomatoes, and sunflowers. Not one but two entries titled "Rub a Dub Dub, Three Babies in a Tub."

Close to four hundred entries in all, hoping to bring home top honors in the nation's oldest baby parade. It's a major production—five categories, thirty-five judges, scores of volunteers, hundreds of contestants, all culminating in a two-hour parade on the boardwalk that may be the Jersey Shore's single most colorful spectacle.

"It's amazing how many people have worked on this over the years," says baby parade chairwoman Doris Dahlhausen. "We've worked on it for forty years."

Rub a dub dub,
three babies in a tub

The Ocean City Baby Parade
might be the most colorful
event on the Jersey Shore.

Her husband, Bruno, was parade director for twenty years; he passed away in early 2002. The parade was founded in the early 1900s by Leo Bamberger and a group of Philadelphia residents who summered in Ocean City. Evelyn and Russell Hanscom ran the parade for thirty years; their son, Russell, still lends a hand.

"I've been coming to this parade seventy-three years," jokes the seventy-three-year-old Hanscom, whose mother was pregnant with him when she was working on the parade.

Past grand marshals have included Joe DiMaggio, Pete Rose, Sally Starr, and Captain Kangaroo. Prizes? "Lovely" silver dishes and bowls, according to Egner.

"If anyone needs water, please take it; don't dehydrate," Evelyn Cain tells contestants minutes before the parade's start. Cain and her sister, Marilyn, were the queens of the baby parade in 1960, becoming the first twins-category winners.

Sailor boy.
Ocean City
Baby Parade

Being on display can be tiring.
Ocean City Baby Parade

Lily's Diner—
that's Lily Rene
Hogan sitting
pretty—won a
first prize.

Twins continue to be one of the parade's highlights; a special award is given to most outstanding twins or triplets.

Tot-sized lifeguard stands and diner interiors, shark fin–decorated wagons, tropical islands on wheels, schoolhouses, and farm stands—all are on display in this baby parade. One mother deposits her two-year-old in a blanket-wrapped cooler—"Keeping Cool in Ocean City" reads the sign—and pulls him down the boardwalk. Another infant sits in a big pot; Mom holds a sign saying: "Today's Special. All U Can Love. Baby Lobster Tail Priceless."

Pulling baby
brother down
the boardwalk

Sounds like a winning formula.

The key plank of one-year-old Paul Callender's "platform"

Hoping for votes, in more ways than one, is Paul Callender, a one-year-old comfortably ensconced in an American flag–decorated red wagon. A sign taped to the wagon reads:

> *Party—My Crib.*
> *BYOBB. Bring Your Own Baby Bottle*

Paul, according to his mom, Susan, is running for governor, even if he doesn't know it. His platform: Free Diapers for All.

The Sedge Island Experience

At low tide, you can walk on water to get to Great Sedge Island, but that would spoil the fun of puttering along in a little outboard across a finger of Barnegat Bay to the twenty-acre main island, which is known as, well, Main Island.

You could bring your own food, but that would mean you'd miss the messy pleasure of standing ankle-deep in the mudflats and pulling up clams for dinner.

You should bring bug spray, because after you eat your clams the greenheads and mosquitoes will have you for dinner.

The little outboard has barely reached the island after the short ride across the bay, and three huge lumps have already risen on the writer's hand.

"The greenheads are really unbearable this year," Tony Raniero, the island's caretaker, will say later. "It's the worst in history as far as the greenheads and common flies."

The main house on Sedge Island

Jim Merritt, director of the Sedge Island program

It's not an outhouse, it's a Clivus.

It's just another weekend on Great Sedge Island, a little-known slice of Jersey Shore heaven located in the middle of boat-choked Barnegat Bay. The greenheads prove to be beatable (it helps to spray yourself head to toe with industrial-strength bug spray). The weather turns out perfect—warm, sunny, breezy. And the food, cooked by Brian Vernachio, director of the New Jersey Audubon Society's Plainsboro Preserve and leader of the small group that has booked the island for the weekend, is abundant and amazing.

The Sedge Islands, located in Barnegat Bay between Island Beach State Park and Waretown, constitute the state's first marine conservation zone. You can't just show up and ask Jim Merritt for a room. Merritt, director of what is known as the Sedge Island Experience, runs the island with a firm benevolence. Think "Survivor" crossed with Gilligan and Mary Ann. There are rules—no Jet Skis or other personal watercraft. No alcoholic beverages (the writer would especially regret this). Radios, TVs, video games? Strongly discouraged. And don't forget to leave the door to the Clivus Multrum (the thoroughly modern outhouse) open and the lid down after you use it.

But if the Sedge Island Experience proves to be miserable, you have only yourself to blame. This is the anti–Jersey Shore: no crowds, no traffic, no boom boxes, no noise except the flutter of bird wings. No convenience stores or pizza joints, but you'll quickly get over that, especially if you have a cook like Vernachio around.

There is something about being surrounded by the Jersey Shore, yet so totally removed from it.

There is something about going to sleep at night and hearing nothing except the sound of the wind slapping your window blinds.

There is something liberating—primeval?—about digging up great dripping gobs of muck as you forage for your dinner.

Clams, scallops, shrimp, crisp Jersey corn, and barbecued ribs make up dinner the first night out. There's cocktail sauce for the shrimp and a hot sauce called Liquid Lucifer.

Someone is curious about hiking through the bush and around the rest of the island. "I choose not to bushwhack because of the ticks and poison ivy," says Kate Cook, a guide working as a summer intern for the state Division of Fish, Game, and Wildlife.

Curiosity satisfied.

She's working here all summer. When Merritt offered her the job, he warned her about the greenheads. "He said, 'They're going to take out chunks of your skin. They'll swarm you if you're wet.'" She laughs. "He made it sound a lot worse than it is. I was ready for World War II with bugs."

A great blue heron squawks on the opposite bank. Two royal terns in attack formation make a "crackkk crackkk" sound overhead. Water laps against the shore. Stars cascade across the night sky. Later, we

Kate Cook, a conservation intern for the state Division of Fish, Game, and Wildlife

will sit on the upstairs deck and watch the Friday night fireworks display at Seaside Heights. Boom, flash, boom, flash. Sound carries so well out here you can hear conversations on boats a quarter mile offshore.

In the late 1800s, early 1900s, the Sedge Islands were better known than they are today. In the mid 1600s, the Board of Proprietors of the Province of East Jersey began purchasing from the Indians the barrier islands from Manasquan to Little Egg Harbor Inlet, an area known as Barnegat. Duck hunters soon found the Great Sedges prime hunting grounds. In 1884 Leonard Warner, founder of Warner Pharmacological Laboratories (now Warner-Lambert), bought the Great Sedges and built a lodge, which he called Sedge House. Among the guests: Presidents Grover Cleveland, William McKinley, and Teddy Roosevelt. Sedge House burned down in 1909. Ownership of the islands would pass from Warner to the Great Sedge Gunning and Fishing Club to James R. Hensler of Toms River, a "big jolly man who seems to have enjoyed every venture in which he was ever engaged," according to *The Great Sedges*, a history by Pauline Miller of the Ocean County Cultural and Heritage Commission. When John A. Hensler, Hensler's nephew, and his wife, Helen, took over the islands, the Sedge "began to swing," according to Miller. Guests in 1940 included Babe Ruth, who sat in a blind with several friends and shot at brant flying overhead. The shots could be heard on radio; the Babe's hunting trip was part of a WOR broadcast called "Exploring Offshore Waters." Later, back at the lodge, the Babe played poker and made clam chowder.

In 1979, the Hensler family sold the Sedges to the state Department of Environmental Protection. The Sedge Islands Marine Conservation Zone, managed by the state Division of Fish, Game, and Wildlife and the Division of Parks and Forestry, now contains 1,200 acres of tidal marsh, the state's largest osprey colony, a nesting peregrine falcon, 200-plus species of birds, and several other collections of islands, including the Busters—Little Buster and Big Buster.

Not everyone comes away enamored with the place. A reporter for a major newspaper who spent the weekend complained about the lack of air conditioning, "which seemed more like a necessity and less like luxury."

Seems like she missed the point of the place. Tony Raniero has been the caretaker since 1996. He and his wife, Jackie, live in a cozy solar-powered houseboat several hundred yards from the main lodge. Tony, a youthful-looking sixty-seven, is off the island once a week—"max." His wife is a more frequent visitor to the mainland, and civilization; right now, she's getting her hair done in Manahawkin. Yes, Raniero says, they have cable. "I get everything, hundreds of channels," he says.

Tony Raniero, caretaker
at Sedge Island

"269 is my favorite; that's the History Channel." They spend the winter at their home in Palm Bay, Florida.

"If I drop dead out here tomorrow," Raniero says, "it would be a pleasure."

Breakfast the next morning: thick, fruity blueberry pancakes and thick, smoky bacon. The third male in the group wears a T-shirt that reads: "If a man speaks in the forest and there is no woman to hear him, is he still wrong?" The day is spent canoeing and hiking and digging for clams. A surreal moment; after two hours silently rowing through the tidal marsh, we pull the boats ashore, climb a dune, and come face-to-face with scores of powerboats on Barnegat Bay.

Vernachio kneels on the beach to give an impromptu lecture on horseshoe crabs. The limulus leech, he says, lives in only one place in the world—the horseshoe crab's gills.

Merritt makes it clear to groups beforehand that the Sedge Island Experience is not a vacation—you're there to learn about the Great Sedges and their place in the preservation of the state's natural resources. It's very much a hands-on experience; participants are expected to crab, clam, and fish.

"People think, 'Oh, we're going to just paddle around from place to place,'" Merritt says. "That doesn't happen."

(For more information, you can e-mail Merritt [sedgeisland@nac.net] or write [Sedge Island, Box 571, Seaside Park 08752].)

Merritt came to the Sedges after seventeen years' working for the New Jersey School of Conservation in Stokes State Forest. He was also a drug and alcohol counselor at High Point High School. "Any kids that got to be a pain in the ass, the vice principal sent them to me before he kicked them out of school," he explains. He loved both jobs but after seventeen years was "totally bored." He's run Sedge Island since the summer of 2000. Groups—Newark teachers, Plumstead Township officials, a Rutgers University outdoors club, the Governor's School on the Environment, among many others—stay here from mid-April to mid-October.

"You can get great weather or really crappy weather out here," Merritt, fifty-seven, says. "April can be nasty. September is beautiful. You're so exposed out here; there's nowhere to hide."

When you first visit Sedge Island, you think: "What am I going to do here all weekend?" When the weekend is over, you think: "I don't want to leave."

"Nobody knows this part of New Jersey exists," Cook says.

From the Indians to Babe Ruth to our select group this weekend, the Sedges continue to cast their solitary spell. Fred Donnelly, a nephew of Helen Hensler's, said it best after a 1954 trip:

> We've had clams and crabs and flukes,
> Food that's more than fit for dukes.
> We've sailed and swam and just slept
> While Bud cooked and shucked and swept.
> Beer, bourbon, wine, and champagne
> All in one day with no strain.
> Though this time we're forced to leave
> To earn our yearly reprieve,
> Some day we will stay at Sedge
> Till they dig us out with a dredge.

The Tent People

A man walks up to the beachfront information booth in Ocean Grove with a look on his face that is half quizzical, half angry.

"Is beer now allowed on the beach?" he asks David Shotwell.

"No," Shotwell replies.

"Well, there is someone over there with one."

Shotwell waves down a town employee on a golf cart and asks him to check it out. No alcohol is allowed in charming, quaint, and stubbornly anachronistic Ocean Grove, founded in 1869 as a Methodist camp meeting site. Another reminder of the resort's religious roots: no one is allowed on the half-mile beach before 12:30 p.m. on Sundays in the summer. That may sound restrictive, but up until 1970, the beach was closed all day Sunday. And until 1980, no vehicles were allowed inside the town's limits.

Old and new.
Ocean Grove

If Ocean Grove seems blissfully out of touch with the rest of the Jersey Shore—it may be the only town with free parking at its beachfront parking spaces—so be it. The people who live and vacation here prefer it that way. That the town is situated next to decrepit Asbury Park makes Ocean Grove, with its neatly swept sidewalks and tidy Victorian homes, appear to be a seaside Brigadoon.

Shotwell, administrative officer for the Ocean Grove Camp Meeting Association, is responsible, more than anyone, for making the town run. The retired director of the Neptune High School band has lived in Ocean Grove since 1956; three of his four children have bought homes in Ocean Grove. Shotwell, a former beach captain here, also is secretary of the United States Lifeguard Association.

The town's centerpiece, its moral anchor, is the Great Auditorium, a magnificent structure that from the inside, with its soaring ceiling and vaulted windows, resembles a great ship. Sunday services, often accompanied by a 200-voice choir and a world-renowned pipe organ, are held here at 10:30 a.m. and 7:30 p.m. Every summer for the past 133 years, the Great Auditorium has hosted a summer concert schedule, with performers ranging from symphony orchestras and string bands to folk singers and doo-wop groups.

There are programs, talks, and lectures all over town in the summer, in such lovingly restored or maintained buildings as Bishop Janes Tabernacle, Grove Hall, and Thornley Chapel (for more information, go to *www.oceangrove.org*).

One of 600 tents available seasonally in Ocean Grove

"There's not much time to relax in the summer," Shotwell says. "To relax, I have to get out of town."

But the town's most idiosyncratic feature is not the Great Auditorium, the restricted Sunday beach access, or the free beach parking, but the tents.

From its beginnings in the late 1800s, Ocean Grove was a tent village. Every summer, thousands of people would spend their summers in mildew-proof canvas tents, "nomadic dwellings cozily ensconced under the foliage," according to a 1887 story in the *Asbury Park Daily Press*. Four hundred of the 600 tents in existence then were owned by the Camp Meeting Association; the rest were "the personal property of their inmates." Tent decor evidenced "the same variety and sometimes lack of taste" found in normal homes.

The tents then cost $75 to $100 for the season. The tents now run upward of $2,500 for "tent" season—May 15 through September 15. The tenters pay for gas and electric, but water is included. There are now just 114 tents, but they are no less delightful.

"We stay until the very end," says Richard LeDuc, sitting in the living room of his tent on St. Paul's Place. "We're about the last ones left every summer."

The twelve-by-seventeen tent he and his wife, Ruth, have rented for the past twenty years is a regular fixture on Ocean Grove Historical Society–sponsored tent tours. "They know we're always available for tours," Ruth says. "They know we're willing. Not everyone is."

"Our feeling is that we're supporting the camp meeting association," explains Rich, a former warehouse manager for Schering-Plough. "One of the ways you do that is to introduce [outsiders] to Ocean Grove."

The town, now part of Neptune Township, was founded by Methodist minister William Osborne. He admired the wide beach, thick groves of pine, cedar, and hickory, and the absence of mosquitoes. Town boosters sold the religious atmosphere ("the preachers were aflame with zeal, enthusiasm, and power," according to one eyewitness account), the seaside serenity, and the ocean bathing.

"The surf lubricates the joints like oil; grave men fling out their limbs like colts in pastures; dignified women, from the very inspiration of necessity, sport like girls at recess," exulted Dr. Aaron Ballard, a charter member of the Ocean Grove Camp Meeting Association.

Visitors here included presidents (Grant, Garfield, McKinley, Taft, Teddy Roosevelt, Wilson, and Nixon) and other distinguished people (Admiral Richard Byrd, Booker T. Washington, Helen Keller).

The abundant peace and quiet, apparently, did not extend to services. "If you want to hear such singing as you can hear nowhere else this side of heaven, go to a live Camp Meeting at Ocean Grove," one preacher told his congregation. "The singing alone is enough to sweep down the powers of hell."

The LeDucs get all kinds of questions during the tours. Can the tents be rented by the week? (No.) Is there plumbing? (Yes.) "They're shocked to see a television," Ruth says.

They are both Methodists, but there is no religious requirement for tent rental. Rich belongs to the Ocean Grove Ushers Association, whose 168 volunteer members work services and concerts at the Great Auditorium. Ruth is president of the ushers association's ladies' auxiliary, which will raise $33,000 this year for organizations in town through plant sales, ice cream socials, fish dinners, and other events. "The ladies do a lot," Ruth points out. "We're a force to be reckoned with."

Some of the "tent people" sleep in the front, tent portion; the LeDucs, who live in Clark the rest of the year, sleep on a canopied bed in the cottage portion. The bathroom is nestled inside the small, sloping-roofed kitchen. There's a refrigerator and microwave, but no oven. Everything appears slightly tilted—the rooms, walls, ceiling.

"It's all built on sand and rock," Rich says. "Everything tilts."

Outside is a small yard and garden. Stitched on the tent flap are the words "Home Sweet Tent." The LeDucs drive home once a week to pick up their mail and cut the grass.

There are rules in tent city. No more than seven people are allowed to stay overnight. No subletting the tent. No pets, and no open fires or barbecues. An air

The cozy interior of the LeDuc tent

conditioner is not allowed unless you provide a doctor's note stating it is medically necessary.

"As far as alcohol is concerned, what you do in your tent is up to you," Rich says. "They don't want you to sit on your porch and drink."

You learn quickly not to speak too loudly or make much noise, unless you want all your neighbors to hear exactly what's going on in your tent.

"Everyone can hear what you say and when you say it," Ruth says, laughing. "You hear people snoring, babies crying."

Rich and Ruth LeDuc's tent. The rocking chairs are chained to posts.

When they moved in, a couple gave them good advice: "If you have a secret, don't tell it in the tent."

Life is not so idyllic that you don't need to keep an eye on your belongings. Tents have been broken into; when the LeDucs had their porch chairs stolen, they chained the next pair to a post. And someone goes around occasionally and absconds with the tenters' flowerpots to sell at the local flea market. A tag under each of the LeDucs' flowerpots reads, "This pot was stolen from the LeDucs."

But, all in all, it's paradise. The LeDucs clear out, reluctantly, every September 15.

"It's a wonderful place to summer," Ruth says.

"We have more friends in Ocean Grove than we do back home," Rich says.

How long will they keep coming down here?

"Forever and forever," he replies.

Jaws at the Jersey Shore

Richard Fernicola, a doctor and a local historian, points to a sinuous curve in Matawan Creek, a stone's throw from the Garden State Parkway and the whoosh of southbound traffic.

"The shark came to this bend," says Fernicola. "That's where the attacks happened. We're not anywhere near the ocean. You can see how weird this is."

In July 1916, something happened here that was so unbelievable, so horrific, that to this day it strains even the bounds of fiction.

Here, in July 1916, two people were killed by a monster that held New Jersey—and much of the nation—in the grip of terror.

"HUNDREDS SEEK TO SLAY SHARK," screamed a headline in the [New York] *Evening Mail*. "THINK MONSTER TRAPPED IN CREEK." From the *Philadelphia Eagle*: "SKIPPERS SAY SEA ALIVE WITH SHARKS."

There was only one killer shark, but it was attacking bathers along the Jersey Shore in a savage, almost supernatural fury.

"This is where Lester floated up," says Fernicola, standing atop a concrete abutment above Matawan Creek.

"Lester" was Lester Stillwell of Matawan, a frail twelve-year-old who was attacked and killed by the shark while swimming with five buddies in the creek on a hot summer afternoon.

Even eighty-five years later, the story of the killer shark, apparently a lone great white, remains scarcely believable. But New Jersey's killer shark episode amounted to the first documented shark attacks in American history. The most famous shark movie of all is said to have been at least partially based on it.

"It happened before!" Chief Brody (Roy Scheider) says in *Jaws*. "The Jersey beach!"

"1916," Hooper (Richard Dreyfuss) replies. "There were . . ."

"1916! Five people chewed up in the surf!"

"In one week!"

Route 109,
Lower Township

Actually, four people were "chewed up" by the monster from the depths in the summer of '16. The victims included two in Matawan and one each in Beach Haven and Spring Lake. Renny Carten, an athletic, broad-shouldered fourteen-year-old, survived the attack, although his chest, according to one account, looked "as if raked by the tips of knives."

"I remember having some friends over for dinner," recalls Michael Capuzzo, a former reporter and writer for the *Miami Herald* and the *Philadelphia Inquirer* and author of *Close to Shore*. "We were sitting out on the deck. I told them the story. Their tongues were hanging out."

The killer-fish tale became the subject of two books—Capuzzo's *Close to Shore* and Fernicola's *Twelve Days of Terror*. Capuzzo's book is the more vivid and dramatic, Fernicola's more scholarly and probing. Taken together, the two provide a full story of the terrifying events of July 1916.

The shark attacks tapped one of the most primal of all fears, according to the authors.

"Of all the predators implicated in man-eating events, none conjures up more intense dread than the shark," Fernicola says. "It is certainly terrifying to be confronted by a bear deep in the woods, or a tiger in a remote village in India. . . . It is quite another issue, however, to imagine being a shipwrecked sailor, a surfer, or a beach bather about to be attacked, dismembered, and consumed by a dark, black-eyed monster with razor-sharp teeth, viselike jaws, and sandpaper-like skin."

The story of the killer shark "is the oldest suspense story of all," Capuzzo observes. "Man killed by monster."

At dawn on Saturday, July 1, the [Engleside] hotel [in Beach Haven]
and the ocean were united by the bright gold band of beach. Men read the
Philadelphia Public Ledger and smoked Turkish cigarettes on the porches,
and discussed the German march to Paris and the fall of the Philadelphia A's
to last place. That was the summer the great Connie Mack affixed to the
American language the axiom "You can't win 'em all." . . . By late morning
the sands were crowded with young men and women in the startling new
swimming costumes, the women revealing inches of leg never before seen in
public. In playful teams, men and women built sand castles, a new art in
America and Europe that year. ——Close to Shore

The great white is known as *Carcharodon carcharias*, from the Greek *harcaros* (teeth) and *karcharias* (shark), sometimes translated as "the biter with the jagged teeth."

"The shark does not come out of the womb, like most fish, as a helpless egg, one of millions adrift in the sea to be plucked by predators," Capuzzo says. Rather, it comes into the world four to five feet long, fifty to eighty-five pounds, hunting. Nature has equipped the shark "more splendidly than anything that lived to find prey," according to Capuzzo. Most of its brain is given over to enormous olfactory lobes; the great white can smell prey a quarter-mile away.

In 1915, Beach Haven had enjoyed its finest tourist season in history; merchants had no reason to believe 1916 would not be better. A more genteel clientele packed the Engleside; a raucous atmosphere prevailed at the new Hotel Baldwin. The Baldwin Grill flowed with beer at all hours; riflemen picked porpoises off in the surf as crowds cheered.

Charles Vansant, a twenty-three-year-old Philadelphian vacationing with his parents and sister at the Engleside, was the shark's first victim, on July 1. Vansant, playing in the ocean with a red Chesapeake Bay retriever, was attacked in three feet of water. First to reach him was Alexander Ott, who later became a swimming showman with Johnny Weismuller. Ott hoisted Vansant under his arms and started pulling him to shore, only to discover, to his horror, that he was in a tug of war with the shark over the body. Other men joined Ott and formed a human chain, dragging the body—and the shark—onto the beach. The shark suddenly turned, and in a whirl of foam, disappeared.

His left leg nearly torn off, Vansant died a half-hour later.

The reign of terror had begun. At first, it was barely news. The *New York Times* gave it four paragraphs on its very last page July 3, two days after the attack.

Charles Bruder was the next victim.

The twenty-eight-year-old bell captain at the venerable Sussex & Essex Hotel in Spring Lake decided to take a quick swim during his lunch break on the afternoon of July 6. It was a hot, languid day; beach-goers dozed under black-and-white-striped umbrellas.

On his way to the water, Bruder told two lifeguards he was "not afraid of sharks." Bruder, an excellent swimmer, was attacked about one hundred yards from shore. The shark tossed him repeatedly in the air—the bell captain's body pin-wheeled above the water—between strikes.

"A shark bit me! Bit my legs off!" Bruder screamed. "He's a big fellow, and awful hungry."

Bruder, mortally wounded, was dragged by bystanders onto the beach. Scores of women fainted when they saw what was left of his torn, mutilated body. "Many persons were so overcome by the horror of Bruder's death that they had to be assisted to their rooms," the *New York Times* reported.

The first coastwide shark alarm in the nation's history was sounded. Within a half-hour, thousands of bathers fled more than thirty miles of beaches "in a shark panic without precedent," according to Capuzzo. "For the first time in American history, people en masse were afraid to enter the water."

Suddenly, sharks seemed to be everywhere. Ben Everingham, captain of the Asbury Park lifeguards—known as "surfmen" at the time—clubbed a shark with an oar while in his rowboat. Twenty boys and girls swimming near the Robbins Reef Yacht Club in Bayonne saw a shark appear off the float extending from the clubhouse. The children ran, screaming, for the bathhouses. Swimmers and boaters as far south as Maryland and Virginia viewed the ocean and the waters of Chesapeake Bay "as something menacing and foreign," according to Capuzzo.

The media response to the Bruder attack was "one of absolute shock and amazement," Fernicola points out. "The Vansant attack of July 1 had seemed like a quiet, if freakish, aberration. But when the unthinkable attack on Bruder occurred in front of hundreds of tourists, including the upper crust of society, the cork burst off the magnum bottle of champagne."

Asbury Park's beaches were barricaded by steel wire. Similar precautions were taken at New York City beaches; no one knew where the shark—or sharks—would strike. "We Are Fencing Our Beach with Wire," advertised the owners of the Manhattan Beach Baths. "Come Down and Laugh at the Sharks!"

Despite eyewitness accounts, many scientists refused to believe a shark was the killer. John T. Nichols, assistant curator of the American Museum of Natural History's Department of Recent Fishes, said the culprit was *Orcinus orca*, the killer whale. Hugh Smith, director of the U.S. Bureau of Fisheries, said it was a swordfish.

Lester Stillwell was the next victim, in a place so unlikely, so unreal. On July 11, Renny Carten, splashing in a swimming hole in Matawan Creek with his cousin, had been badly scratched and scraped by a creature neither boy could identify.

The next day, Stillwell and five buddies removed their clothes and dove off a dilapidated dock at the old Wyckoff steamboat landing in Matawan. One moment, Stillwell was floating peacefully on the water. The next, he was screaming, his arm held fast in the mouth of what one of the boys, Charlie Van Brunt, called "the biggest, blackest fish" he had ever seen.

Young Stillwell "was shaken, like a cat shakes a mouse, and then he went under," according to one of the boys. For one terrifying second, he reappeared, shrieking, then disappeared under the water for good.

The local constable rounded up a group of men and marched them to the creek. The men plunged repeatedly into the water. After a while, they gave up. One of their number, Stanley Fisher, a strong, athletic, twenty-four-year-old tailor, decided to give it one more try. Suddenly, Fisher screamed; he had found Stillwell's body. The next moment, the shark, lurking nearby, attacked. Three or four times, it pulled Fisher under. He finally worked himself free, but most of the flesh between his hip and right knee had been ripped off.

A doctor, not believing Fisher would survive a trip in a car to the nearest hospital in Long Branch, had him placed on a stretcher and carried to the Matawan train station, where Fisher and an attendant waited an hour for the next train. The ride took two and half hours; Fisher was brought, still conscious, to Monmouth Memorial Hospital. Five minutes after he was placed on an operating table, he died from massive blood loss and shock.

The townspeople went into a shark-hating—and baiting—frenzy. Sticks of dynamite were tossed into Matawan Creek. "Many believed they saw sharks moving after each blast," the *New York Times* reported. Women armed with shotguns patrolled the banks.

Acting Mayor Arris Henderson posted a $100 reward for the shark. "The above reward will be paid to the person or persons killing the shark believed to be in Matawan Creek," the notice read. "In the event there is more than one shark killed, a pro rata sum will be paid for killing each shark."

Unknown to everyone, the shark had fled.

A glance at any newsstand would reveal that Matawan had catapulted to the national limelight. The town was the object of widespread curiosity and sympathy. The shark was the object of widespread infamy. The foreign battles of World War I could not hold a candle to the bizarre excitement surrounding the rampaging man-eater from the sea. The hungry press was writing with pens already red hot from the previous two attacks. This was a horror novel being played out in real life, the ending yet unknown.

—Twelve Days of Terror

The frenzy spread throughout New Jersey, and up and down the coast. The Chamber of Commerce in Paterson—not exactly near the ocean—offered bounty money for captured sharks. "Wildwood offered the generous reward of $1,000 for any proven man-eater, but to meet the criteria, the shark had to contain human remains when dissected," Fernicola says.

Crewmen aboard a Maryland State Police schooner reported "big sea monsters" in Annapolis harbor. A Tampa, Florida, boater said sharks in the Gulf of Mexico were so thick, he returned to port. Letters to newspaper editors, according to Capuzzo, advocated that Washington send the entire U.S. submarine fleet to destroy the shark. President Woodrow Wilson turned to Treasury Secretary William Gibbs McAdoo to lead "a war on sharks."

By mid-July, the war on sharks was "the biggest news in the *Washington Post* and front-page headlines across the world—in New York, Philadelphia, Chicago, even London," according to Capuzzo. The Jersey Shore economy was in crisis; guesthouse bookings from Cape May to Spring Lake were off 75 percent.

On July 14, two fishermen, Michael Schleisser and John Murphy, cast off in a boat from South Amboy. An hour later, in Raritan Bay, their boat suddenly slammed to a halt. Something huge was caught in the net. Shark! It rose out of the net and onto the stern, snapping its jaws. With a broken oar that he had thrown into the boat as an afterthought, Schleisser, a renowned animal trainer and big-game hunter, clubbed the shark to death. He and Murphy towed it back to South Amboy.

Back in his Harlem row house, Schleisser cut open the shark, finding what later would be confirmed to be human bones.

The killer shark's reign of terror was over.

"It was as if the culprit was caught with a smoking gun, walking down the street of the scene of the crime," Fernicola says.

The shark was placed in the front window of a New York City newspaper; a mob of 30,000 people gathered. There were gasps and cries of "Monster!" The carcass of the fish, according to Capuzzo, disappeared shortly after it was displayed in the window; some years later, a scientist spotted its jaw hanging in the window of a Manhattan storefront before it disappeared forever.

> In an era of fisheries that would eradicate it, science that would plumb all its mysteries, and global media that would reveal its every move, the great white endures in the depths where it has always reigned: in cautionary tales told by mothers and fathers, in whispers in the unconscious, in offshore shadows, and in ripples on a tidal creek.
>
> —Close to Shore

Charles Bruder, the bell captain, is buried at Atlantic View Cemetery in Manasquan. Charles Vansant is at rest in South Laurel Hill Cemetery outside Philadelphia. Lester Stillwell and Stanley Fisher, the killer shark's last two victims, are buried at Rose Hill Cemetery in Matawan. A simple granite marker identifies Stillwell's grave. It reads: "Lester Stillwell. 1904–1916."

Wacky Golf

It's come down to this—a short putt for par late at night on the fourteenth hole of a miniature golf course in Leonardo. The two golfers have battled head to head all day in a tournament that started early this morning in Cape May, proceeded to the Ocean City and Atlantic City boardwalks, and stopped at a fiendish little course on Long Beach Island before ending at the Hole in One Miniature Golf Course in Leonardo.

It is a classic professional and personal battle, a showdown between writer (of a Jersey Shore book) and publisher (of a magazine devoted to pinball machines). The publisher, behind all day, has this short putt to draw within two after sixty-seven holes of golf. The publisher is looking for revenge; he lost a similar competition the previous year to the writer, a contest that if not for his total collapse at the fiendish little course on LBI would have been decided by a mere three strokes—726 to 729.

The publisher—Tim Ferrante of *Game Room* magazine—looks his putt over, strokes it cleanly—and misses. The look on his face says "I am going to throw myself in front of traffic on Route 36," but he says nothing.

What is there to be said? The match is over. Four holes left, three shots ahead, the writer has no intentions of blowing it.

Lacey Nicholl lines up a putt at Tee Time, Ocean City.

Goofy Golf,
an Ocean City
miniature golf
course

"The sun has set on your game," the writer told the publisher the year before as he closed out the Jersey Shore Mini-Golf Invitational, a two-day, five-county, fifteen-course, 270-hole miniature golf marathon stretching from Cape May to Whitehouse Station. This year's tournament would be scaled down—one day, five courses—but bragging rights would be established for another year.

For most people, fortunately, miniature golf is fun, not cruel and unusual punishment. There are ten thousand miniature golf courses in the United States, more than seventy in New Jersey. We couldn't play them all, and we certainly would not come close to matching Edward Sullivan's feat in the 1930s, when miniature golf was in its heyday and course owners tried to outdo each other with promotional stunts. Sullivan played 146 hours straight for the title "World's Champion Miniature Golfer." The only known song written strictly about putt-putt is called "I've Gone Goofy Over Miniature Golf." And millions of us have.

Yes, it's not the most demanding of sports. It may not even be a sport. "The feeblest outdoor activity this side of waiting for a bus," someone once said.

Blame it on James Barber, of Pinehurst, North Carolina. In 1916, Barber hired Edward Wiswell to lay out on the grounds of his estate a mini-course incorporating all the elements of "real" golf. When Wiswell was done, Barber looked at the postage stamp–sized course and pronounced, "This'll do!" The course became known as Thistle Dhu.

But it remained behind the closed gates of Barber's estate. It was up to entrepreneurs like Drake Delanoy and John Ledbetter, who in 1926 built New York City's first outdoor miniature golf course on the roof of a skyscraper in the financial district. The duo went on to open 150 rooftop golf courses in the city.

The 1920s found Americans "dizzy with new prosperity and leisure time," according to Nina Garfinkel and Maria Reidelbach, co-authors, with John Margolies, of the wonderful, witty *Miniature Golf.* The suffrage movement gave women "social license to pursue activities outside the home that were previously considered unacceptable." These and other factors led to the wacky fads for which the decade is famous: dance marathons, Ouija boards, flagpole-sitting, hot dog eating contests—and miniature golf.

By 1930, there were between twenty-five thousand and fifty thousand miniature golf courses in the United States. Back then, obstacles took many odd and creative forms. "Jungle" courses featured live animals, including, at one course, a tethered bear and a monkey, both trained to snatch balls from players. At one Los Angeles course, dragons and Chinese junks floated in the water and an eight-piece orchestra played.

Communities across the nation, according to Garfinkel and Reidelbach, were "driven crazy by the Madness of 1930." In East Orange, more than one thousand people turned out for a town council debate on night and Sunday play. The marines were called in to build a course at Camp David. Department stores offered mini-golf fashion lines.

Not everyone loved the game. Towns, driven by residents' complaints of mini-golf players causing commotion on courses well after midnight, sought to regulate closing times. Even the Mob was alleged to have infiltrated miniature golf. Chicago tabloids told of attempts by Al Capone's gang to organize the city's 300 courses and exact thirty-five-dollar "initiation" fees. The sport nearly evaporated in the early thirties, victim of legal restrictions, burdensome license fees and taxes, a worsening economy, and market saturation.

But miniature golf, drawing on the baby boom and the growth of suburbia in postwar America, experienced a revival in 1950s and remains strong today. In the summer, Jersey Shore mini-golf links are packed with children and adults; many courses hold weekly tournaments. And the International Olympic Committee has accepted mini-golf as a provisional sport for the 2004 Olympics in Athens, Greece.

Harris Miniature Golf Courses Inc. in Wildwood is the nation's largest builder of mini-golf courses. The folks here get all kinds of questions. How much does a miniature golf course cost? How many water and other hazards should it include? Real rocks or fake rocks? Should the course be difficult, easy, or somewhere in between? And then there are questions that come from way out of bounds.

Helpful sign, The Sand Trap

"One guy called and asked if we could build a course on a submarine," vice president Pat Boylan says, laughing.

The company's answer?

"Uh, no," Boylan notes.

If you dream it, the people at Harris will build it. The company constructs forty to fifty miniature golf courses a year. The majority are in this country, but Harris courses can be found in the Bahamas, Grand Cayman, and Cyprus. A "low-end" course will cost about $200,000, according to Boylan. "Most courses you're looking, lit and landscaped, for $250,000 to $300,000," he explains. "With caves on it, you're looking at $300,000 and up."

The company, started in 1957 by Joe Harris, a local handyman, and now owned by Rich Leahy, has built more than four hundred courses worldwide. Courses generally take four to six weeks to finish. Harris employs six five- or six-man construction crews; an additional fifteen people work in the office, where a bucket of balls is always on hand for impromptu miniature golf contests.

A mini-golf course generally requires a half- to three-quarters of an acre. They can be built just about anywhere, with the possible exception of a submarine. There are Harris courses at Fort Sill, Oklahoma; an Indian reservation in North Carolina; inside a dome in Thunder Bay, Ontario; atop a former landfill in Auburn Hills, Michigan; and at South of the Border in South Carolina. Harris courses in New Jersey include Garden State Golf Center in Branchburg, Jersey Springs (FunMania) in Old Bridge, Cape May Miniature Golf, and Atlantic City Miniature Golf.

"We're trying to take miniature golf to the next level," says Boylan, mentioning a miniature golf manual, the first of its kind in the industry, being developed for course owners. "We have designs in the works for exploding volcanoes and tiki huts."

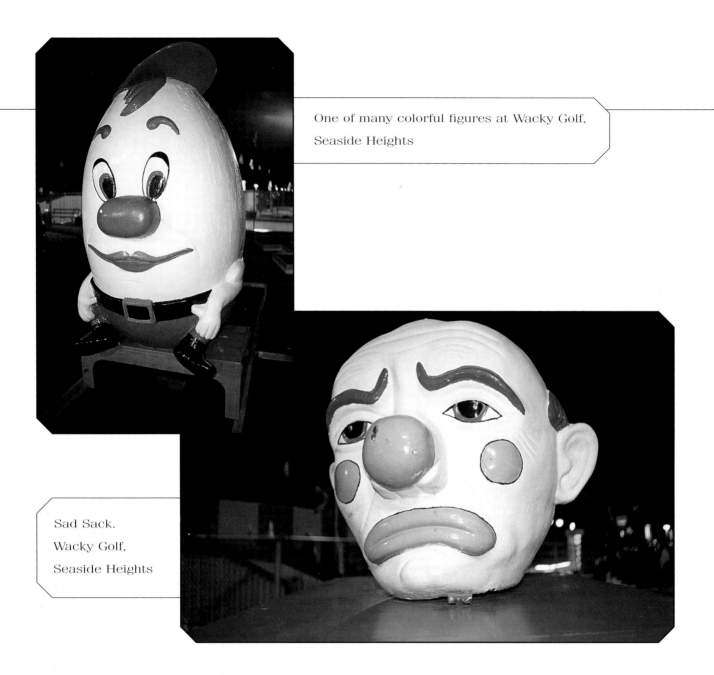

One of many colorful figures at Wacky Golf,
Seaside Heights

Sad Sack.
Wacky Golf,
Seaside Heights

A sampling of Jersey Shore miniature golf courses from north to south:

MONTEREY MINIATURE GOLF
Route 35 North, Monterey Beach, Dover Township

If some of the holes here lack verisimilitude—"Brooklyn Bridge" looks more like a row of picket fences than the famous bridge—the course is another old-fashioned treat. Windmills, tin cups, bright red walls, plus scoring tables and pens at every hole. Pay once, play twice before 5 p.m.

WACKY GOLF
Casino Pier, Seaside Heights

There may be no more fun course in New Jersey than Wacky Golf, which spreads across five rooftops above the Seaside Heights boardwalk. Colorful figures—Humpty Dumpty, an elephant, giraffe, zebra, tiger, skunk, jack-in-the-box—provide the obstacles. An added feature: 25, not 18, holes. Wacky Golf, a vivid reminder of putt-putt's colorful past, may be low on challenge, but it's great eye candy.

ROSSI'S GOLF COURSE

Twentieth and West Central avenues, South Seaside Park

For a real time-warp experience, pay a visit to Rossi's, near the entrance to Island Beach State Park. Red-and-white windmills, little red schoolhouses, pink castles, and white whales dot the course. Straight out of the 1950s.

SAND TRAP

Twenty-third Street and Long Beach Boulevard, Ship Bottom
(609) 494—3185

It looks so cute and innocuous, with abundant flowers and shrubs and a fifteen-foot-high replica lighthouse. But a closer look reveals the Sand Trap as a fiendishly clever little course, with sinuous swirls and ridges, especially around the cups.

ATLANTIC CITY MINIATURE GOLF

Boardwalk and Mississippi, Atlantic City
(609) 347—1661

"Play 18 holes of world-class golf at Atlantic City's premier miniature golf course." It's also Atlantic City's only miniature golf course. Great views of boardwalk and beach, and well-maintained, but only mildly challenging.

Whoops! The Sand Trap, Ship Bottom

Teddy Mishura keeps score at The Sand Trap.

If only it were that easy.
The Sand Trap

JUNKYARD GOLF
1336 Boardwalk, Ocean City

Junkyard Golf—many of the hole lips are in need of repair and the scorecard is the size of a business card—looks like it should be resigned to a miniature golf course scrap heap. But if you're looking for mini-golf in Ocean City without maxi lines, play here. Nice views over the boardwalk and beach. Obstacles include a tiger, rhino, flashing lighthouse, and, on one hole, the unlikely combination of a church and front-end loader. You'll really have to mess up to exceed the five-shot per hole limit.

CONGO FALLS
1132 Boardwalk, Ocean City
(609) 398–1211

Adventure-type courses—with caves, erupting volcanoes, and crashed airplanes and helicopters—are the rage in the mini-golf world these days. Congo Falls,

Lacey Nicholl,
Tara Whalen,
and
Luke Nicholl,
Tee Time,
Ocean City

which encompasses two courses, can be a refreshing place on a hot day, with its raging waterfalls and rushing streams. The holes are strewn with multiple humps, bumps, and ridges.

TEE TIME

642 Boardwalk, Ocean City

Cute, colorful, old-fashioned course, with lots of twirling, spinning obstacles—stars, Ferris wheels, windmills, propellers, even Barney Rubble feet.

PUTTER'S BEACH

Sixty-third and Landis Avenue, Sea Isle City

Putter's Beach, with its bright blue putting surfaces, is pretty, but pretty boring. The surface is something called OmniGrass, "acclaimed as the most realistic sports surface available," according to a sign. "None of the holes are too long or unnecessarily complicated," according to the course's web site (*www.puttersbeach.com*). No kidding.

TEE TIME

239 Ninety-sixth Street, Stone Harbor

(609) 967–5574

Rooftop course, "one of only five American tournament standard courses in the United States and one of only two courses within 2,000 miles that is sanctioned by the World Mini Golf Federation as an approved certified course for tournament play," according to its web site (*www.seven-mile-island-com/tee_time_miniature_golf.htm*).

SEAPORT MINIATURE GOLF

Boardwalk and Schellinger Avenue, Wildwood

(609) 522–3900

Boring course, and the same stupid pirate keeps singing "Yo-ho-ho" over and over. But the course, which winds around a water park, offers great views of the Ferris wheel, boardwalk, beach, and ocean. Obstacles include turtles, wood beams, and a shipwrecked boat. "Mountain climbing is not allowed," according to the score-card, although we didn't see any mountains.

CAPE MAY MINIATURE GOLF

Jackson and West Perry streets, next to Swain's Hardware, Cape May

(609) 884–2222, *or go online at www.capemayminigolf.com*

"You can go around twice; you can go around three times if you want," the friendly owner tells us at Cape May Miniature Golf. "I can see you're golfers."

Appearances can be deceiving. The Harris course bears such company traits as waterfalls, multiple levels, and winding holes. Course record: 32.

STOCKTON GOLF

Beach Drive and Howard Street, Cape May

(609) 884–4036

A small, beautifully landscaped course, right across from the beach, dotted with English holly, rose of Sharon, and other greenery.

Little Miss Chaos

Braden Kessler walks hesitantly across the stage in the Music Pier auditorium in Ocean City, teetering toward an unlikely collection of props. Pots, pans, forks, spoons, a xylophone, a cowbell, and plastic toys are arranged in a little circle, awaiting their master's bidding.

Kessler stands motionless, looking at the pots and pans as if they are about to do her serious harm. Clearly, she is not in the mood, and Mark Soifer does not want to prolong her paralysis.

"Thank you," he says into his microphone.

Little Braden exits stage right, but not before picking up the cowbell and tossing it into the audience.

Little Miss Chaos has struck again.

A Little Miss Chaos contestant bangs away.

Meghan Berry, right, and Andi Cocozza dressed up as Raggedy Ann and Andy.

"It's for people who always wanted to compete at a beauty pageant but missed the bus," Soifer cracks.

Wait, that's not Little Miss Chaos, that's Miss Miscellaneous, another of the strange but true events held during the single nuttiest week of the Jersey Shore summer—Weird Contest Week in Ocean City.

Saltwater-taffy and French-fry sculpting contests; the Little Miss—and Little Mister—Chaos competition; the Miss Miscellaneous pageant, and a wet T-shirt contest are all part of Weird Contest Week, generally the second week in August.

Wait a minute. A wet T-shirt contest in Ocean City, which proclaims itself "America's greatest family resort"?

Sure. Only this wet T-shirt contest consists of contestants' taking a wet T-shirt and seeing how far they can throw it. Miss Miscellaneous pits young girls exhibiting offbeat talent and outrageous costumes against one another. At the Little Miss and Little Mister Chaos competitions, the winner is whoever makes the most noise.

"We like to give three- to five-year-olds things to do they really like to do," Soifer explains. "Instead of dressing up in pretty costumes, banging on pots and pans."

Weird Contest Week once included a blueberry pie–eating contest, but it was discontinued because pie-gorged entrants had the habit of tossing their berries. So it was replaced with the Artistic Pie Eating Contest, testing not who ate pie most artistically, but who made the most artistic pie. There were rockets made of pies, desk lamps made of pies, and a Chiquita banana made of pie. The pie contest has since been replaced by the saltwater-taffy and French-fry sculpting contests, all part

Stop being a hot dog! Ocean City

of Soifer's continuing effort to get Ocean City to live up to its reputation as a fun, family place.

"It's a good idea to add something to these events every year," says Soifer, who has been Ocean City's public relations director for thirty-plus years.

The wackiness in Ocean City goes well beyond Weird Contest Week. There's the Doo-Dah Parade, in April; the Ocean City Baby Parade, the nation's oldest, in August (see "Free Diapers for All" chapter); the Freckles Contest; and the Miss Crustacean Pageant and Hermit Crab Races in late July, a delightfully bizarre competition in which

Sitting pretty, Ocean City

There she is, Little Miss Chaos! Heather Schroeder, right, wears the crown.

hermit crabs are dressed up in tiny costumes and paraded on miniature floats, then later race to see who's the fastest hermit crab at the Jersey Shore (the 2002 winner finished in 13 seconds, not far from the all-time record of 6.3 seconds set by Hermie, who has since gone "to the Great Hermit Tree Crab Sandbar in the Sky," according to Soifer).

And don't forget the Quiet Festival, held in November, which is already a quiet time of the year.

"It's all quiet stuff," Soifer explains. "Mime storytelling, leaf rattling, feather dropping."

The craziness began in the early 1980s, when Soifer launched the Miscellaneous Suntan Contest. There were categories for best-tanned left arm, best-tanned soles of feet, a Count Dracula category for palest face, and a miscellaneous category "for anything people wanted to show us within the limits of propriety."

But the contest was discontinued after a TV piece that some felt made the city look silly. That led to the blueberry pie–eating contest, which didn't last long.

No one is danger of losing her lunch at any of the current events. The worst that can happen? A Little Miss Chaos contestant flaunting tradition and not making any noise, or throwing a cowbell off the stage. This year's winner: Heather Schroeder, who shakes the xylophone, bangs on the pots, and whacks her spoon several times on a Dutch oven pan.

"We're all done here," her mom says, escorting her daughter offstage.

Katie Berry of Mount Laurel—Little Miss Ocean City in 1999—and Amanda Waldner of Cherry Hill win the Miss Miscellaneous Pageant with a song-and-sort-of-dance routine, "You've Got a Friend in Me," while Michael Brown of Ocean City wins Mr. Miscellaneous with his Sponge Bob Square Pants imitation. Prizes? Crowns, scepters, necklaces.

And then everyone joins in the official Miss Miscellaneous theme song:

> *Miss Miscellaneous, so, so spontaneous,*
> *Never extraneous,*
> *Even if it would rain on us,*
> *It wouldn't be a pain to us,*
> *Because we adore you, we adore you,*
> *Miss Miscellaneous.*

"The theme is wacky but not tacky," Soifer says of Weird Contest Week, in its fifteenth year.

The city public relations director is seventy, so he'll get paid for being weird only a few more years. How would he like to be remembered?

"I did my job, and people had a good time," he says.

Hold My Beer While I Kiss Your Girlfriend

"Las Vegas and Disneyland are two of the tackiest places on earth, but Las Vegas and Disneyland are beautiful; Wildwood is just tacky," says Jack Morey, sitting on a five-dollar wing chair in the lobby of the StarLux in Wildwood.

The StarLux, with its sweeping, space-agey facade and plastic palm trees, is the coolest crash pad in this town of neon-lit, retro hotels and motels.

Morey owns the StarLux. He does not own Wildwood (the name most people use to describe Wildwood, Wildwood Crest, and North Wildwood); it only appears that he does. The Morey Organization, of which he is executive vice president, owns nine motels, several restaurants, and three piers. Wildwood—with the state's most colorful, kinetic boardwalk (thirty-eight blocks long) and impossibly wide, free beaches—is the greatest show on the Jersey Shore. Always was, always will be.

StarLux, Wildwood

Hey, ice cream man.
Wildwood

Budding sandcastle builder,
Wildwood

Its future? Ask the guy with several days' stubble wearing shorts, baseball cap, and a T-shirt that looks like it would perfect attire for the local tiki bar.

"Wildwood," Morey says, "is better than Disney World."

Millions of Americans would disagree, but the Wildwood Crest resident is neither starry-eyed visionary nor fast-buck developer. Sure, he has a stake in Wildwood's future, but his family had a big part in the resort's past. Wildwood was built on fantasy and fun; Morey's late father, Will, built a gaudy empire of candy-colored hotels and ride-studded piers back in the fifties. Will Morey's first hotel, in 1953, was the aptly named Fantasy. He built or acquired more than thirty hotels—the Flagship, Satellite, Sea Chest, the Carousel. In the late 1960s, he turned his attention to the Wildwood boardwalk, then a collection of inexpensive kiddy rides and gritty dance halls. With his brother, William, he bought a failing seaside bar and opened Morey's Pier, which initially featured just a giant Fiberglas slide

Wildwood

and a towering replica of King Kong. By the early 1980s, Morey's domain grew to include two more amusement piers and two water parks.

But Shore-goers started to discover Atlantic City, Cape May, Long Beach Island, and other beach destinations. Wildwood was a night out, but no longer a place to stay for a week. By the 1980s what once looked cool looked chintzy, and many of the hotels, like the resort itself, were showing their age. The 1970s and 1980s, according to one account, were "rough and tumble, a time when, as some locals remember it, anyone who could reach the bar could get a drink."

The resort's low point, Morey says, came in the late 1980s. "There was no convention center, no hope," he points out.

The resort started to rebuild—and recast its image. Morey and the late architect Steve Izenour were among those who saw potential for a nostalgia gold mine in the old hotels and motels. Today, the Wildwoods may not be all the way back, but developers and investors have had the resort on their radar screens for some time. Hotels and

Rio Motel, Wildwood

motels are now selling for two or three times what they were worth ten years ago, according to Morey.

Ahh, the hotels. Wildwood is a blast from a dig-it past, a Magic Kingdom of Kitsch with dozens of cool 1950s and 1960s motels from the So-Bad-It's-Good school of architectural design. The Caribbean, with its winding, head-spinning central staircase. The Waikiki, with its thatched-roof entrance. The Crusader, fronted by a pavilion locals call the "Ivanhoe tent." The Eden Roc, its roof lit by multicolored spaceship lights. The pagoda-shaped Singapore, the tiki-torched Tangiers, and the Satellite, topped by stars and miniature Sputniks. The Jolly Roger and its sword-wielding plastic pirate. The Imperial and its curvy—dare we say voluptuous?—balconies. The one and only Ebb Tide, where the lower floor juts in and the upper floor juts out.

Morey, forty-one, formed the Doo-Wop Preservation League in 1997 to preserve the town's vintage commercial architecture. Some prefer the terms Space Age, Jetsonian, or Populuxe to describe Wildwood's architectural look. Morey likes Doo-Wop because it recalls the music of the time.

In the summer, the Doo-Wop Preservation League (*www.doo-wopusa.org*) runs trolley tours of this seaside Kingdom of Kitsch, focusing on the Caribbean, StarLux, Jolly Roger, and other motels along this stretch of Beach Blanket Bingo land.

The owner of the pagoda-roofed Singapore was inspired by a trip to the Orient to come up with his "incredible concoction," a guide will tell you. At the Pink Champagne, champagne glasses are painted on every room door. Dig the tiki head on the spear sign outside the Tahiti.

Morey; Chuck Schumann, captain of the Big Blue Sightseer Cruise; doo-wop enthusiast Michael Zuckerman; and others coined names for categories of the time-warp architecture: Blast-Off (futuristic-looking hotels such as the

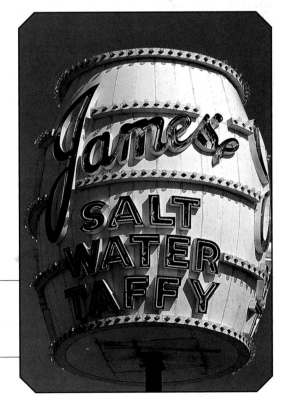

Don't leave without buying a box. Wildwood

That's not a pizza, it's a UFO. Wildwood

Fantasy, Admiral, and Satellite); Vroom! (hotels "built for speed," with lean-in, lean-out walls and angled roofs, such as the Ebb Tide and Rio); Pu-Pu Platter (hotels with the thatched hut/ tiki head/outrigger look, such as the Tangiers and Tahiti); and the Phony Colonee style, ersatz-colonial buildings (Saratoga, Sand Castle) that were definitely not built before the American Revolution.

There is a street in Wildwood named after Bobby Rydell, whose grandmother had a house here. Rydell's recording of "Wildwood Days" ("Every day is a holiday and every night is Saturday night") was number 17 on the *Billboard* charts in June 1963. Everyone from Ella Fitzgerald and Dave Brubeck to the Supremes performed in Wildwood. A purple shopping bag on display in the Doo-Wop Preservation League museum (3201 Pacific Avenue, 609–523–2400) describes the former Rainbow Room, where Chubby Checker performed, as "the birthplace of the Twist."

Other businesses in town have jumped on the Doo-Wop bandwagon; a Subway across the street from the StarLux sports a curvy, Jetsonian orange sign.

Morey talks about plans for a surf/skateboard park, a 200-foot-high roller coaster, more and better rides, even a museum devoted to boardwalks worldwide and to Wildwood. New sidewalks and signage along Rio Grande Avenue, the major thoroughfare into the Wildwoods, have been added. A new convention center on the boardwalk is open.

Wildwood itself, however, still needs work. There are vacant storefronts in the forlorn downtown business district. Even Morey concedes "you wouldn't want to stay in" some of the hotels that are in need of renovation.

And there are signs Wildwood may fall victim to its own retro success. Dozens of hotels are slated to be torn down. Motel owners are getting upward of $50,000 per unit; a thirty-room hotel could fetch $1.5 million. An alarmed Greater Wild-wood Hotel-Motel Association identified a hit list of hotels scheduled for demolition: The Ala-Kai. The Catalina. The SurfSide. El Capitain. And the delightful, absolutely-one-of-a-kind Ebb Tide.

As all that kitsch hangs in the balance, Wildwood continues to exert its dizzying draw on high school and college students, firefighters (the state firefighters' convention is held here every September), seniors, and others. If you run out of things to do here in a day or two, you need to check for a pulse. There is a head-spinning schedule of events, everything from the East Coast Stunt Kite Championship and the National Marbles Tournament to the Polka Spree by the Sea and the United Way Rubber Duckie Regatta.

Best show at the Jersey Shore? No contest. Wildwood is an eight-year-old's ultimate summer fantasy. Rides everywhere—flashing and screaming past you. Roller coasters and Tilt-a-Whirls, bumper cars and the Himalaya. Endless games—spinning wheels, break the bottle, ring-toss, 23 Skiddo, pinball. Sounds exploding everywhere—buzzers and bells and beeps and bangs. More food than you could possibly eat in a summer—sizzling sausage sandwiches, fat Philly cheesesteaks, gloriously greasy thin-crust pizza. Fortunetellers, clairvoyants, and palm readers. Miniature golf until two in the morning. Buy a tacky T-shirt ("Hold My Beer While I Kiss Your Girlfriend"). Get your body pierced and then walk a few steps to the Boardwalk Chapel (see "Boardwalk Chapel" chapter) and contemplate the error of your ways.

"Pick out a prize!" shouts a barker at Fat Daddy's Lucky Games. "All you have to do is win it."

Jellyfish Attacked My Face

There are many grueling athletic competitions at the Jersey Shore every summer, and we don't mean the impromptu drinkfests at the beachfront bars.

There are the All-Women Lifeguard Tournament in Sandy Hook, the Bridge-to-Bridge Row in Barnegat Bay, and the ocean inner-tube race in Point Pleasant, among others.

But the toughest day you can spend at the Jersey Shore is finishing—or surviving—the annual Atlantic City Around-the-Island Swim, a 22½-mile endurance contest in which Vaseline-covered competitors fight cold, choppy water, strong currents, hypothermia, exhaustion, and the occasional jellyfish in the face.

"Got a massive one in my face," says Shelly Clark of Australia, popping grapes into her mouth as she sits in the medical tent post-race. "It just planted itself there. I thought it was seaweed. Then it stung. Yah!" She points to angry red welts on her arms and legs. "There, there, there, just in the last ten minutes."

The various obstacles—disregard any shark sightings, you're not likely to encounter Jaws in the back bay—make the Around-the-Island Swim one of the more demanding events on the open-water circuit.

The race began on a dare. In 1954, two Atlantic City lifeguards jumped off Steel Pier into the ocean and proceeded to swim around Absecon Island. Over the years, the event was transformed into the Around-the-Island Swim, attracting top open-water swimmers from around the world. Local competitors in recent years have included Margate native Jim Mucciarone, a Navy Seal, Tiffany Swain of South Orange, and Samantha Chabotar, a high school Spanish teacher.

"A lot of people say this is one of the hardest marathons in the world," Chabotar, a former member of the Atlantic City Beach Patrol, recalled before the 2000 race. "There are so many different elements: the ocean, bay, tides, and winds. If you ask me, it's one of the hardest sporting events of all."

"The toughest swim in the world" is how 2002 Around-the-Island Swim director Mike Giegerich describes it.

Australian Shelly Clark spreads some good old medicated goo.

Contestants lather up with various jellyfish-, chafing-, and sunburn-repelling ointments.

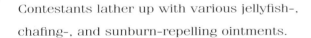

Former Atlantic City Mayor Jim Whelan competed in the swim in 1979; in fact, he swam the entire course in the early seventies in an attempt to revive the event, which had been halted in 1964 because of declining interest.

Behind him, the eight swimmers competing in this year's [2002's] swim (total purse: $18,000) go through their last-minute preparations. Mostly it consists of greasing themselves head-to-toe with various sunburn-, chafing-, and jellyfish-repelling ointments.

It is Clark's third Around-the-Island Swim and her fourth open-water race in the past month. She won a race in Quebec, finished second in another there, then won a cross–Long Island Sound competition.

Her goal here? "To finish in eight hours." The course record is six hours, fifty-four minutes, set by Stephane Lecat of France in 2001. The women's record is seven hours, fifty-one seconds, set by Shelley Taylor-Smith, like Clark an Australian, in 1992.

Even training for a race like this is grueling. Clark swims six to seven hours every day and spends several hours in the gym three or four times a week lifting weights.

"I'm doing a fair few races this year," Clark explains. "I'm doing ten; it's my first [full] year."

The Around-the-Island Swim isn't exactly a must-see event on anyone's Jersey Shore calendar, and Whelan can't understand why.

"The people associated with this are frustrated, because it hasn't generated interest, except among hardcore fans," he says. "It hasn't gotten the coverage it warrants. But it does have a place. Here's an event that has a world-class locale and field."

This year's race lacks several marquee names, including Lecat and Claudio Pitt of Argentina; they are competing in an open-water race in Macedonia this weekend. Clark started on the open-water circuit in 2000. The Around-the-Island Swim was her first event. How did she do?

A youthful spectator, Around-the-Island Swim

"Went to the hospital," she replies. "Dehydration and exhaustion. Got caught in the current."

Each swimmer is accompanied by a rowboat, manned by two rowers and a trainer. Each rower gets one hundred dollars and a T-shirt. According to Gail Otten, Igor Majcen's trainer, the Around-the-Island Swim is the only race of its kind that is manually assisted; in all other races, crews make their way around in powered boats.

Trainers feed their swimmers during the race. Otten supplied Majcen with Power Gels (liquid carbohydrates) mixed with Gatorade and Pepsi Cola.

"I've worked with swimmers who wanted Coca-Cola, bananas, and Cheerios," she says, laughing.

At Gardner's Basin, where the race begins and ends, spectators drape their legs over the sea wall and glance at the water for sign of the swimmers. This year's swim turns out to be a head-to-head battle between Majcen of Slovenia and local hero John Kenny, of the Atlantic City Beach Patrol.

"We have just learned John Kenny is making his move on Igor; it'll be a battle right down to the wire," race announcer Jim Craine tells the crowd.

But Majcen outlasts Kenny; the Slovenian swimmer finishes in seven hours, fifteen minutes. "I'm fine," he says, clambering atop the dock, where he is instantly wrapped in a blanket and escorted to the medical tent. Kenny, exhausted, his face puffy, does not respond at first when paramedics dockside ask him how he is feeling. In the tent, he lies on his back, motionless, his eyes flickering, But twenty minutes later, he is up and about. He is happy with his performance; this is his fourth marathon race, and his best finish.

"The last four, five miles were real tough," he says, grabbing a piece of watermelon from a bag. "I was fighting the current the whole way."

Behind him, swimmers help themselves to a post-race spread of pizza, tacos, chili, hoagies, bananas, grapes, and chocolate eclairs.

"I feel little aches and pains," Majcen, thirty-two, says. "My shoulders and arms are sore. The first night [after a race] you don't get much sleep. You roll around in the bed. You have to wait for the second night."

Clark finishes in eight hours, twelve minutes. She will be back for next year's race. Why does she swim marathons as opposed to shorter distances?

"I'm better at this," she replies. "You know how much I wish I was a fifty-meter swimmer? Your race is over in twenty seconds."

Up next for her: a ten-kilometer race in Atlantic City in two weeks, then the world open-water championship in Egypt at the end of September.

In the meantime, plenty of food, and even more rest.

"I'll probably take tomorrow off," John Kenny says of his beach patrol job. Probably?

"Definitely," he says, smiling.

The Mayor of Sunset Beach

There are many great places to watch the sun go down at the Jersey Shore. The Seagull's Nest in Sandy Hook. Atop Barnegat Light on Long Beach Island. Dockside at Gardner's Basin in Atlantic City.

But the best show of all might be at Sunset Beach, west of Cape May, north of Cape May Point, adjacent to Higbee Beach.

Just look for the concrete ship *Atlantus* moored eerily and permanently several hundred yards offshore, or for the cars parked along Sunset Boulevard.

Hundreds of people gather on the beach at sundown every day for the Sunset Beach flag ceremony. Kate Smith sings "God Bless America" as volunteers lower the American flag and the sun slides below the horizon. Parking is free, but Marvin Hume figures you might spend a few dollars in his three gift shops and Beach Grill on Sunset Beach, part of Lower Township.

"I've been doing this for twenty-nine years," Hume says at the end of another flag-lowering ceremony.

Call him the mayor of Sunset Beach; he owns the property and concessions and supervises the flag ceremony. All the flags are veterans' casket flags donated by the families. The people who help him lower the flag each evening are eager volunteers; you sign up for flag duty on a calendar behind the counter in the main gift shop. This mid-July evening, nearly half of the volunteer days for next summer are already filled in.

"Every flag flown here is flown with pride and honor," Hume says.

Hume is a vet; he served in the Navy Air Force in the South Pacific during World War II. He and his crew would repair or strip damaged planes. "When planes became shot up and smoking, they didn't like to let them land on the carriers, so they went into the drink," he explains. The planes would then be towed back to the nearest American-occupied base or island.

"It was kind of hot sometimes," says Hume, and he doesn't mean the weather. "The Japanese had us zeroed in with their mortars."

He lost his two closest friends at Pearl Harbor, one on the *Arizona*, one on the *Oklahoma*.

When he returned home, he worked for an aircraft builder in St. Louis. In 1957, he opened a science and nature gift shop on the Atlantic City boardwalk. One day, the owner of a gift shop on Sunset Beach walked into Hume's store and asked him if Hume could supply him with some animal skulls. Not long after he asked Hume if he wanted to buy the Sunset Beach place. Hume bought the store and expanded Sunset Beach over the years, adding two other gift shops and a restaurant. His two daughters and son-in-law work here full-time. But his passion clearly lies in the flag ceremony, generally held from April through October.

"We'll do it by request in the dead of winter," the eighty-one-year Lower Township resident says.

A special guest earlier this summer was retired Brig. Gen. Paul Tibbets, who as pilot of the B–29 *Enola Gay* dropped the bomb on Hiroshima on August 6, 1945. Tibbets gave a "stirring" speech to the 1,500 spectators, according to Hume.

The mayor of Sunset Beach has missed just a few flag ceremonies over the years. "I've had nine operations, for various things, at the veterans' hospital," he explains. "They got me in pretty good shape now."

The most memorable flag ceremony occurred twenty years ago, in a thunderstorm. "Thousands" of lightning bolts danced on the horizon as the words "the bombs bursting in the air" from "The Star-Spangled Banner" rang out.

"The most dramatic thing we've ever experienced," Hume says.

The shops are open daily year-round (see *www.sunsetbeachnj.com*) except on Christmas and Thanksgiving. But the highlight of Hume's day comes at sundown, when the crowd gathers on the beach and Kate Smith begins to sing.

"There are a lot of tears shed here," he says quietly. "A lot of people have lost loved ones." His eyes mist over. "I love this flag."

A Banner Season

Gathered next to a battered old van straight out of the post-apocalyptic landscape of a Mad Max movie, Mike Barchi, Meredith Fisher, and the rest of the ground crew watch the skies at Allaire Executive Airport in Wall. It is a brutally hot July afternoon; the sun sears your eyeballs and sweat turns your T-shirt into a soggy rag. No wind, not a cloud in the sky.

Perfect day for a banner pilot.

Matt Applegate, the one-legged manager of the Aerial Sign office at the airport, is up in the sky. So is Dan Corle, whom everyone calls "Daytona Dan." As is Frank Barchi, Mike's brother, an autoworker at the Ford Motor Plant in Edison, who has been a banner pilot for twenty years.

They all work for the Hollywood, Florida–based Aerial Sign, the nation's largest aerial advertising company. Cruising several hundred feet above the water from Sandy Hook to Cape May, banner pilots keep you up on the latest dinner and

The Aerial Sign ground crew members watch banner planes at Allaire Executive Airport.

Scott Barchi, son of banner pilot Frank Barchi, looks for Dad's plane.

Matt Applegate, manager of the local Aerial Sign operation

drink specials at restaurants and bars, band lineups at nightclubs, wireless phone offers, special events, and other useful beach news.

It may look boring from the ground—back and forth, back and forth—but banner pilots talk in reverential tones about their seasonal work.

"This is fundamental flying at its best," Jim Goggin, a fifty-two-year-old banner pilot from Pompano Beach, says back at the hangar. "Stick and rudder flying." He points at his Piper Cub. "That's my office window."

Down in the oven-baked field, Mike Barchi supervises the banner pickup. Banner pilots do not take off and land with a banner; they snag each banner off posts set eight feet apart in the field, using three-prong grappling hooks attached to the plane. Good pilots can snag the banner first time out; others might need

three or more attempts. In a summer-long tournament, Aerial Sign pilots tried to see who was the best "picker-upper." You missed one banner, you were eliminated. Today, it had come down to two pilots— Applegate and Frank Barchi, who each had picked up forty-odd banners without missing one.

The banners, 200–300 feet long, are attached to 300-foot-long sections of rope. They are arranged neatly in rows in the field, waiting for pickup. Mike Barchi's crew includes Fisher, a College of New Jersey junior majoring in law and justice. Weekends,

Ground crew member
Meredith Fisher

Easy for you to say.

Daytona Dan

the crew's day begins at seven a.m. and doesn't end until five or six p.m. Weekdays, it's generally nine to five.

About forty–fifty banners will go up on a good day; the pilots first fly south to Seaside, turn around and head north along the shoreline to Sandy Hook, then fly inland back to the airport. Each pilot will tow six to eight banners a day.

The banners leave the ground with a snap and are dropped with a whoosh and rustle. Fisher, Steve Canares, and other ground crew members quickly retrieve the banners, rolling them up in neat little packages and stacking them near the beat-up old van for reuse.

For the pilots, the plane of choice is the Piper Super Cub, which can chug happily along at the slow speeds—forty, forty-five mph—essential to banner flying.

"They're built just for this," explains Mike Barchi. "Extended wings, high-horsepower engine. Means they can fly low and slow."

"You want an airplane that's very docile, an airplane that flies very good at slow speeds," says Ron Booker, a self-described employee "of a Department of Justice agency" who stopped at Aerial Sign today to begin his week-long training as a seasonal banner pilot.

Many of the pilots live in Florida; they fly up here in the summer, stay with friends or in a company apartment, and head back home after Labor Day. Aerial Sign pays its pilots twenty-five to thirty-five dollars an hour.

Aerial's banners are not just for Jersey Shore bars with $1 shot specials; national accounts like Snapple, Tanqueray, and Cingular Wireless are regular customers.

After their last banner, the pilots trudge back to the hangar to kick back and help themselves to beer from a cooler.

"I've got to go or I'll be in trouble," says Applegate, whose daughters' names are painted on the side of his two airplanes.

He walks halfway to the door, reconsiders, and pulls a beer out of the cooler. "She has only a few more weekends to get mad at me," he says of his wife.

Frank Barchi is smiling; he won the summer-long banner pickup tournament earlier when Applegate finally failed to pick one up.

Out in the parking lot, Goggin changes from the trunk of his car. The Pompano Beach resident had spent most of the weekend towing a Snapple ad back and forth over Boston.

"After thirty years, every time I get in a plane I start smiling," he says.

Daytona Dan is the last one to land. (Actually, he doesn't live in Daytona, but nearby Port Orange.) The North Carolina native has worked for a grocery chain for several years, going from bagger to cashier to management. He's flown banner planes for the past six years.

"Every other job, it's a routine, it never changes," the twenty-five-year-old pilot explains. "Here, each plane flies different. The conditions are different. Banner flying is probably the best flying you'll ever do."

Jersey Shore Haven

A young woman in a van comes tearing up the gravel road in the campground.

"Slow down!" Karen Bence shouts.

"Five mile an hour speed limit!" adds Mary Ann Izzi, pointing to a sign along the road.

The young woman, three children in back, slows down, a sheepish look on her face. Bence and Izzi sigh and continue their conversation. The woman in the van is not long for the campground, anyway. She can't spend the night here, not in that van.

"When everyone is here, this place is still quiet," marvels one regular.

Welcome to Jersey Shore Haven in South Seaville, Cape May County, the best-kept secret along the Jersey Shore. It's the sole Airstream-only campground in the state, a tree-shaded slice of paradise devoted to the shiny aluminum trailers that are the ultimate in streamlined design, the epitome of camperly cool.

Mary Ann Izzi, a host
at Jersey Shore Haven

Karen Bence of Bayonne spends her summers at Jersey Shore Haven.

An Airstream, kicking up gravel, rumbles past, a middle-aged couple inside.

"How long will they be here?" Bence asks.

"One night," Izzi replies. "They're going to see if they like it."

"They'll be here a week," Bence says knowingly.

Nearly one hundred Airstreams and their owners spend their summers here. Shareholders in Jersey Shore Haven pay $875 a summer for rent; nonshareholders pay $1,300 a summer. Sure beats a timeshare at the Shore. A lot quieter, too. Tree-shaded lots, big swimming pool, a picnic pavilion (scene of ice cream socials, seafood dinners, and pizza nights), and "the cleanest bathrooms in the state," according to one resident.

Bence, who lives in Bayonne and is a school nurse in Hoboken, comes down with her husband, Robert, in early June, and stays all summer. Does she ever go back to Bayonne?

"Only if my daughter calls and screams, 'Mom!'" she says, laughing. "I'm so used to the city and hustle and bustle and stress. You come down here, it's so relaxing."

She and her husband and Mary Ann and Al Izzi are Jersey Shore Haven's hosts and hostesses; they take turns running the property, three days at a time. Many of Jersey Shore Haven's habitués are true "geriatric gypsies," roaming the country in their sleek Airstreams, spending summers in Jersey or Pennsylvania, winters in Florida or the Southwest.

Where do the Izzis lives? Everywhere . . . and nowhere.

"We have a Michigan mailing address, a Phoenix area code, belong to the Elks Club in Bismarck [N.D.], my dogs get their shots at a vet in Fort Collins [Colo.], and we belong to the Wally Byam Metro in Detroit," Mary Ann Izzi explains.

Dottie Maier pedals through Jersey Shore Haven.

An icon of American design, the Airstream is still rolling along—more than seventy years after Wally Byam, a shepherd's son, started building trailers in 1931. Byam, who led Airstreams on dozens of goodwill missions overseas, including a Cape Town-to-Cairo caravan in Africa in 1959 and a 34,000-mile trip through Europe and Asia in 1964, preached a gospel of travel, fellowship, and fun. The bullet-shaped Airstream, so named because it rode along the highway "like a stream of air," was the perfect vehicle for its expression.

Among Haven regulars is Gerry Bloch of Woodbury, the oldest person to climb Yosemite National Park's fabled El Capitan—he did it when he was a mere eighty-one.

"I'm an outdoorsman, a rugged type," says the eighty-two-year-old Bloch, who, despite his thin, slightly stooped figure, could run rings around most of us. "I do crazy things, like rock climbing. I've gone skydiving six times, all between the ages of seventy-two and seventy-six. I've climbed the highest mountain in forty-eight states. I have not climbed Mount McKinley; the thin air bothers me."

Not all Airstream owners are as vigorous as Bloch, but they've all been around.

"We've been in every state, many of them several times," says Herb Hitchner of Bridgeton, who bought his first Airstream in 1958. He and his wife, Esther, have driven to Alaska twice in an Airstream, in 1984 and 1994.

"We've been to Banff, Lake Louise, Jasper [in Canada]," he adds, sitting in his comfortable, cozy trailer. "We've been to Yellowstone, Yosemite, through the Bad-lands, Mount Rushmore. . . ."

Among the younger generation of Airstream owners are Somerdale residents Jake Kovalchek and his wife, Michelle, who spend their summer weekends at Jersey Shore Haven with daughters Brielle and Samantha and Dakota, their Lhasa apso. They own a thirty-one-foot 1967 Airstream.

"They're the best," Jake Kovalchek says. "I'm a mechanic. I feel they're the best-quality trailer you can buy. Sure, they're more expensive, but they're worth it."

"You go down the road and, because of the aerodynamics, you don't even know it's behind you," Michelle Kovalchek says.

In terms of design, mystique, and aura, few American inventions can match the Airstream. Both kitschy and elegant, boxy and stylish, Airstreams have achieved near-mythic status in American popular culture.

"There is such a sense of mystery and romance to these trailers," explains Bryan Burkhart, co-author of *Airstream: The History of the Land Yacht*. "With their streamlined design, they evoke a period that is very stylish."

Byam took aluminum-alloy trailer bodies built by aviation designer William Hawley Bowlus and turned them into the first Airstreams, which soon featured iceboxes, electric lights, chemical toilets, and dry-ice air conditioning.

Airstreams have always carried a certain cachet, but, in the past few years, they have popped up everywhere—and not on just on the American interstate. Lucy

Two ways to go. Jersey Shore Haven

Liu's character in the movie *Charlie's Angels* lived in one. Tom Hanks, Sean Penn, and David Duchovny own Airstreams. MTV replaced the Winnebago it had been using on its "Road Rules" series with an Airstream. Ralph Lauren confirmed the Airstream's coolness when Polo.com announced it would sell custom-made, fourteen-foot Airstreams for $150,000 each. And who could forget the alien flying saucers doing battle with the earthling Airstreams in *Mars Attacks,* the 1996 movie by Tim Burton?

Under township ordinance, Jersey Shore Haven residents must vacate the campground by November 1. By Labor Day, many are heading south for Florida Airstream campgrounds. One, in Punta Gorde, is called Paradise.

Robert Bence, Karen's husband, is in charge of the pool at Jersey Shore Haven. The couple lives in a thirty-four-foot 1991 Airstream. Robert is restoring a 1971 Airstream he bought new for $10,000, a package deal that included a 1969 Lincoln. The Lincoln is long gone, but Bence's Airstream will live on.

"I lived in an Airstream fulltime in a Bayonne [trailer] park for twelve years," Bence says. "I raised my daughter in this one. Lot of memories here."

About sixty thousand Airstreams are on the road; eleven thousand Airstream owners worldwide belong to the Wally Byam Caravan Club International (WBCCI), which hosts caravans and rallies throughout the year. New Jersey Airstream owners can belong to one of three WBCCI groups—the Jersey unit, the Delaware unit, or the Watchung unit. Many members offer "courtesy parking" at their homes for fellow members. The WBCCI web site is at *www.wbcci.org.* The official Airstream web site is *www.airstream.com.*

Living in the lap of RV luxury will cost you, though. The smallest Airstream production model,

Even the Tin Man likes it here.

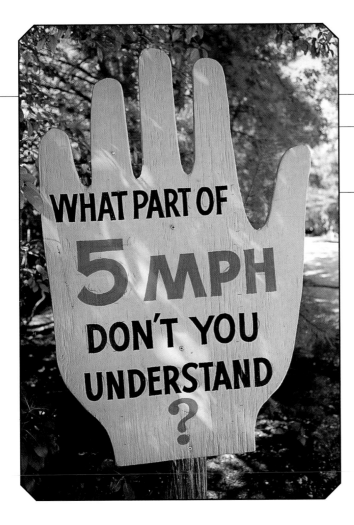

Slow down!
Jersey Shore Haven

the nineteen-foot Bambi, sells for about twenty-seven thousand dollars; the longest, the thirty-four-foot Limited, complete with fireplace, goes for about seventy-five thousand dollars. For many aspiring Airstream owners, used is the way to go; the Kovalcheks bought their 1967 Airstream several years ago for one thousand dollars.

"I'm not a snob about Airstreams," says one owner. "I'm the same guy I was when I had a pup tent. They just look good—and last longer."

"Best trailer on the market for towability," says Al Izzi. He and his wife are on their fourth Airstream. Only drawback? "Aluminum is a dead metal. Once you ding it, you're stuck with it."

There are six red stars painted on the top of Jerry Bloch's Airstream; each star represents five years' membership in WBCCI.

"I'm entitled to one more star, but I haven't gotten around to putting it up," says Bloch, a thirty-seven-year WBCCI member and widower, who lives in the trailer with Buffio, his Siamese cat.

The sign for the campground out on Dennisville Road says "Land Yacht Harbor," which confuses the uninitiated. One visitor pulled up and wanted to know where the boats were.

And there are some who want to turn Jersey Shore Haven into, well, the Jersey Shore.

"There are people who come in here, want to chop down the trees, put up streetlights, pave it over, and turn into a mobile home community," one regular frets.

Airstream owners may be cooler than other RV owners, but at campgrounds, they have to observe the rules like anyone else. "WHAT PART OF 5 MPH DON'T YOU UNDERSTAND?" reads a sign at Jersey Shore Haven.

The worst transgressor of the speed limit, according to one resident? A ninety-two-year-old man.

On Patrol
with the Marine Police

Sgt. Harry Vliet pulls his twenty-two-foot Boston Whaler alongside a low-slung blue-and-white houseboat nestled against a dock in Manasquan. Bikes are latched to the roof; chairs, desks, lamps, crates, boxes—it looks like a waterborne yard sale—are stacked on the deck. A banner reads: "Bateau Humanitaire"—goodwill vessel.

"He says he's on a humanitarian mission from Quebec to Haiti," Joe Carlino of the Coast Guard station in Manasquan tells Vliet.

"He's going to Haiti on that?" asks Vliet, dumbstruck.

"Quebec to Port au Prince," Carlino replies, smiling.

"The French Connection," Vliet laughs.

Vliet exchanges pleasantries with Carlino, whom he knows, and pulls away from the dock. It'll be up to the Coast Guard to verify the Bateau Humanitaire's mission, and judge the vessel's seaworthiness.

The owner of this boat said he was on a humanitarian mission from Quebec to Haiti.

Sgt. Harry Vliet, assistant station commander, New Jersey State Police marine unit's Point Pleasant station

For Vliet, it's just another day on the water. He's the assistant station commander of the New Jersey State Police marine unit's Point Pleasant station. Instead of patrolling the state's highways, this state trooper patrols the waterways around Point Pleasant—the Manasquan River, Metedeconk River, and Barnegat Bay, places like Kettle Creek, Havens Cove, and Seaweed Point. Formerly called the marine police, the state police's marine unit enforces state law on the water; the Coast Guard enforces federal law.

There are five marine unit stations along the Atlantic Shore: Bivalve, North Wildwood, Atlantic City, Point Pleasant, and Sea Bright. Other stations are located at Burlington (responsible for the Delaware River north to Trenton), Port Newark (Newark Bay, the Arthur Kill, Kill Van Kull, and Raritan Bay west of Keansburg), and Lake Hopatcong.

For the forty-eight-year-old Vliet, an Edison native who as a kid spent summers down here and worked as a lifeguard on Monterey Beach in the mid-1970s, the marine unit is a dream job. He has been assigned to state police barracks in Colts Neck, Edison, and Fort Dix, served as a bodyguard for former governor Thomas Kean, and did plainclothes duty in the Atlantic City casinos, but it's clear he loves his waterbound office most of all.

"Unlike [on land], a lot of people don't understand the rules of the road out here," says the chiseled-jawed Vliet, gun holstered at his side. The Boston Whaler, powered by a 175-horsepower Johnson engine, bounces across Barnegat Bay. "They sometimes don't realize they're breaking the law."

Speeders? Technically, you won't find them on the water.

"There are no speed limits out here," Vliet explains. "The only place where there are speed limits is Lake Hopatcong."

But a marine unit officer can ticket someone for operating a boat in a reckless fashion, or "in a manner which unnecessarily interferes with the free and proper use of any waters, or unnecessarily endangers other craft therein or the life or limb of any person upon any craft or in the water," according to regulations.

Other regulations enforced include those on no-wake zones, personal floatation devices, signaling devices (flares), and right-of-way. Vliet and his fellow troopers work boat arsons and drug cases; investigate stolen vessels; pull up floaters, people who have drowned and risen to the surface; and enforce drunk-driving laws (all the stations are equipped with Breath-a-lyzers). In the winter and fall, about twenty-five thousand boats operate in New Jersey waterways. In the summer, the number swells to two hundred thousand or more.

The marine unit, whose jurisdiction extends to three miles offshore, operates a mini-flotilla of boats out of each station. The biggest boat at the Point Pleasant station is a fifty-five-foot, diving platform–equipped craft used for offshore missions. Also tied up in Point Pleasant is a small boat owned by the state Division of Taxation.

"They check on taxes, people's homes," Vliet explains. "They check by land, they check by water."

Out on the water, he gives this reassurance to his passenger: "You get the Whaler swamped, it will not [sink]," he says of the boat, whose Fiberglas hull is impregnated with foam. "If you go overboard, just hold on to it. It's the world's biggest life preserver."

This trusty Boston Whaler is part of the station's fleet.

He steers the boat under the Route 35 bridge between Brielle and Point Pleasant Beach. Two Jet Skiers notice the boat, with its state police markings, and quickly slow down. They look over, anxiety on their faces. Not to worry; they're not doing anything wrong.

Several boaters wave at Vliet as he makes his round. 'You don't get that on the road," he says, grinning. "You get pulled over, it's 'I know he's going to give me a ticket.'"

Several racing boats, here to compete in the Offshore Grand Prix, are on the river. One owner, testing his high-powered craft, gives Vliet a thumbs-up. The trooper attends the pre-race meetings, telling the drivers "what I will and won't tolerate" during their test runs.

Vliet attended Middlesex County College and Frostburg State College. A friend of his dad's was a state trooper. "Ex-marine, a squared-away guy," Vliet recalls. He took the state trooper exam in 1979. "Four months later, I was in the state police academy getting yelled at and screamed at, woken up at five in the morning." He smiles. "Haven't regretted it one bit."

The boat, now in the bay, starts rolling side to side in the choppy water. "This is what we call a confused sea," he says. "Waves coming from all directions."

Twenty minutes later, he coasts into a popular local hideaway called "F" lagoon, a watery version of the tailgate party. Scores of boats tie up here side by side on weekends, as kids go swimming and dad pops open a cold one.

Waterfront business

The state Division of Taxation keeps a boat at the Point Pleasant station.

When Hurricane Floyd punished Central Jersey in September 1999, the marine unit deployed men and boats to the scene.

"We saved more than one hundred people that night," Vliet says. "Waking people up in a second-floor bedroom, they didn't realize their first floors were flooded."

He bounces past a lavish home on an island in the middle of the bay, off Normandy Beach. Vliet's been in the house several times. "Fire alarm kept going off; we had to investigate," he says.

Later, back at the station, he secures the boat and gases it up. In the summer, he works sixty hours a week. He wouldn't have it any other way.

"I like boats, I like the water," he says. "This is a natural."

When Vliet's grandfather died, his ashes were scattered off the jetty in Point Pleasant Beach. You get the feeling Harry Vliet might just put that in his will, too.

Surfer Girls and Boys

It is a golden August morning on the Jersey Shore. Great weather for swimming, sunbathing, bicycling, walking, jogging, anything outdoorsy.

Anything, that is, except surfing. The conditions are terrible. No wind, and waves so flimsy they wouldn't wet a fly. Inside his Ocean Hut Surf Shop, Tony Giordano has just told a freckle-faced thirteen-year-old and his mom the bad news. "If you want to rent a surfboard, I'll rent you the surfboard," Mom tells her son. But Giordano persuades them not to rent the board; conditions are awful, and he knows the kid's going to have a miserable time out there.

Tony Giordano, owner, Ocean Hut Surf Shop

Ocean Hut, located on Route 35 in Dover, just outside Lavallette, is an information center and clearinghouse for Seaside Heights–area surfers. Giordano, who tries to surf every morning before work, opened the shop in 1973. Seaside isn't exactly Honolulu, but it is regarded as one of the top surfing destinations on the East Coast. In fact, *Surfer Magazine* listed it as one of the top ten surf towns in the country, along with towns in Hawaii, California, Florida, North Carolina, and Rhode Island. Seaside's reputation as a surf city is not something new; in the sixties, Casino Pier was a surfing hot spot.

Waiting is the hardest part.

Lacey Nicholl,
Tee Time,
Ocean City

Badge check booth,
Seaside Heights

Tiki Murph sign,
Barnegat

Big Ernie's Diner,
Wildwood

Miss Tiki,
Barnegat

Madam Marie's establishment, Asbury Park

Ocean Grove, where you're not allowed on the beach until 12:30 p.m. on Sundays

Delaware State Parks Beach Patrol team,
All-Women Lifeguard Tournament, Sandy Hook

Beach cleaner,
Seaside Heights

Hubba Bubba, a k a Mike Eremus,
Clownfest, Seaside Heights

RV paradise.
Jersey Shore Haven,
South Seaville

Trump Taj Mahal,
Atlantic City

Island girls,
Ocean City Baby Parade

It's all about the shoes.
Clownfest, Seaside Heights

Happy tenters, Ocean Grove

Surfer girls,
Ocean City Baby Parade

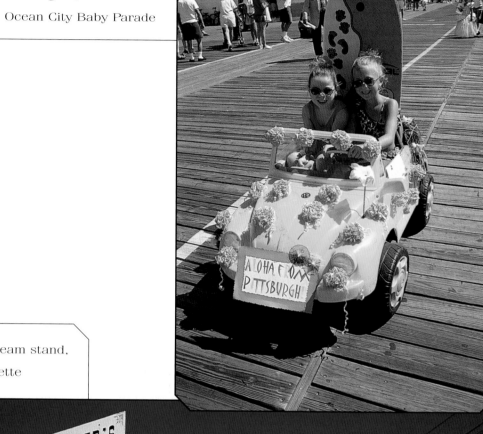

Ice cream stand,
Lavalette

You always
get to be
the tomato!
Ocean City
Baby Parade

Looking good. Miss Deckadance
contest, Atlantic City

Seashore variety store,
Long Beach Island

Edwin Forsythe

National Wildlife Refuge

The Palace,

Seaside Heights

Seaside Heights boardwalk, night

Bonky G Bird and admirer,
Clownfest, Seaside Heights

God made
clowns
just for fun.
Seaside Heights

Contestant,
Ocean City
Baby Parade

Checking things out,
Harvey Cedars

Catch a wave, any wave.
Ocean City

"It was and is one of the best places to surf in the United States," says surfer Sam Hammer of Lavallette, ranked twenty-second in the world.

Twenty, thirty years ago, Giordano was living Hammer's life. Giordano attended the University of Miami—"for barely one semester," he says, grinning. "I called my dad, told him, 'I saved you some money.'"

He opened Ocean Hut when he was nineteen. In the winter, he would take his earnings and surf in Hawaii. In 1977, he finished fifty-second on the world surfing tour. The year before, he placed fifth at the East Coast championships. He surfed in France, Spain, the Caribbean, and Hawaii. He surfed "J-Bay"—Jeffrey's Bay, South Africa, a famous point break (where waves wrap around a promontory and peel as they break).

Bruce Brown's *The Endless Summer*, about two surfers roaming the world looking for "the perfect wave," was released in 1964; Giordano's endless summer lasted right through the seventies.

"I've been all over the world, competing, surfing everywhere," he says.

These days, his surfing is done at the Jersey Shore. Popular surf spots include the Manasquan Inlet, Harvey Cedars, and Ocean City.

The Ocean Divas are a group of women surfers who hold charity events and try to build interest in surfing among girls and young women.

"All I want to do is surf," says diva Joannie Sapienza of Manasquan, a nurse practitioner at Robert Wood Johnson Medical Center in New Brunswick. "It's insane. I just want to surf."

Women make up about 15 percent of all surfers. The number of females who surf swelled by 120 percent from 1999 to 2001, making surfing the second-fastest

Surfer girl,
Ocean City

Danny Muller and Katie Pietrosante.
Ocean City

growing sport for women, according to Board-Trac, a market research firm. In 1997, the East Coast Wahine Championship attracted 76 competitors; in 2002, it drew more than 250.

Winter often provides the best conditions, and Sapienza, like other dedicated surfers, is out there, in her wetsuit.

"If I couldn't surf in the winter," Sapienza told *The Star-Ledger,* "I'd be in a padded cell."

Surfers in Seaside can check conditions year-round on the Ocean Hut web site (*www.oceanhut.com*). A typical report:

> *Wave height: 2–5 choppy*
> *Wind direction: northeast*
> *Tides: L 8:30 a.m. H 2:30 p.m.*
> *Water temp.: mid-60s*
> *Outlook: May clear up before dark tonight. Peace.*

The shop gets one hundred to three hundred phone calls every day, mostly about surf conditions. The report is given live; there's no recorded message. "We're old school," Giordano explains. "We want people to ask a question and get an answer."

Perfect surfing conditions? "South swell coming in from a storm in the Atlantic about three hundred miles away, with a high-pressure system in place giving us offshore winds," he says quickly.

That day is clearly not today. Maybe tomorrow. Mother Nature may not be a surfer, but she will eventually take care of those living the endless summer.

The Stone Pony

"How did I end up here?" asks Domenic Santana, sitting on his brand-new bike outside the Stone Pony in Asbury Park. "It was all on a lark."

Five years ago, the Havana-born Santana—his family came to this country in 1962, when he was eight—drove down from Jersey City, where he lived, to Asbury Park.

"Growing up, that's all you heard of, Asbury Park," he recalled. "But the day I came down here—man, that was a surreal experience. It was like a bomb blew up. You didn't see people or cars. All that was missing were the tumbleweeds."

He drove past a decrepit whitewashed building at the corner of Ocean and Second. "For Sale" signs were plastered on the wall. He called his wife and asked her, "Do you know a place called the Stone Pony?" She did; Santana didn't.

Mural at the Stone Pony celebrates a Springsteen album cover.

155

Domenic Santana, owner,
The Stone Pony

He read up on the legendary rock club's history. Over the years, many big-name acts had played the Stone Pony stage: the Allman Brothers, Wilson Pickett, the Ramones, Jimmy Cliff, Graham Parker, Joan Jett and the Blackhearts.

And, of course, Bruce. Bruce Springsteen did not get his start at the Stony Pony; his first two albums had already been released when the club opened in 1974. But he has played the Pony more than any other venue, appearing there seventy-plus times.

Santana sensed potential at the corner of Ocean and Second. He had grown up in Jersey City; his scarred lip is a reminder of the time he was stabbed on the way to school. He worked as a busboy at the VIP Diner in Jersey City and the famous Stork Club in New York City. His father ran a supermarket at Ninth and Grove. In 1995, Santana opened the Hard Grove Cafe, a popular restaurant.

He saw the crumbling building in Asbury Park and tried to get other people to share his dream. Some thought it delusional fantasy.

"I had to do a lot of convincing of people," he says. "The banks didn't want to touch Asbury Park."

Cookman
Avenue,
Asbury Park

The Stone Pony started as the Magic Touch, a bar. The original owners were Robert "Butch" Pielka and John "Jack" Roig. They renovated the bar and renamed it the Stone Pony; Pielka said the name came to him in a dream (see the excellent book *Rock & Roll Tour of the Jersey Shore*, by Stan Goldstein and Jean Mikle).

The first bands played Top 40 music, then "Southside" Johnny Lyon and his group, the Blackberry Booze Band, started playing three nights a week. A friend of Lyon's, Steve Van Zandt, joined the group, which eventually became Southside Johnny and the Asbury Jukes, the club's first house band.

Palace
Amusements
facade,
Asbury Park

Casino,
Asbury Park

In the summer of 1982, Springsteen played almost every Sunday night at the Stone Pony. He kicked off the "Born in the U.S.A." tour at the club on a hot June night in 1984. By the 1990s, "the Pony's luster had begun to fade," according to Goldstein and Mikle. In 1991, a series of drunken-driving lawsuits forced the Stone Pony into bankruptcy. In 1992, Steve and Judy Nasar reopened the club; Soul Asylum, Blink 182, and other bands played there in the nineties. The club shut down in 1998, reopened briefly as Vinyl, a dance club, and then shut down again.

And that's when Santana drove down to Asbury Park. When he told the city manager he wanted to invest in the city, the official replied, "I wouldn't."

Santana did anyway. The club was in terrible shape. "It was bad, really bad," he recalls. "Pipes—we had 368 leaks. Water gushing behind the walls. It was horrible."

A crew worked around the clock on renovations to meet the Memorial Day 2000 reopening deadline. Then-governor Christie Todd Whitman made an appearance. The Stone Pony was reborn.

Santana moved to Asbury Park, buying a house just blocks from the Stone Pony. "I didn't want to be labeled an outsider, a carpetbagger," he explains. This time, he didn't have to convince the banks but his family. When his younger daughter, Victoria, saw the city for the first time, she said, "Daddy, this is for dead people."

Several years ago, officials offered to relocate the Stone Pony to the old city power plant. Santana said yes. The club's devoted fans were outraged. They sent him 70,000 letters and e-mails protesting the move, and Santana ended up changing his mind.

In the summer of 2002, the city council unanimously passed a $1.2 billion redevelopment plan that would call for 2,500 new townhouses and condominiums, the rehabilitation of 500 existing housing units, and the construction of a 100-room hotel on a vacant piece of land between Palace Amusements and the Casino.

It was only the latest in a series of grand plans to "save" Asbury Park. A decade ago, an ambitious waterfront development plan collapsed in bankruptcy; the most

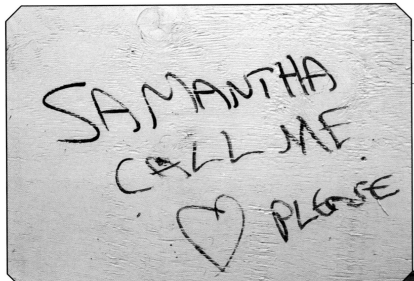

Asbury Park

Sign in front
of Net's Lane
restaurant,
Asbury Park

visible sign of the failed project, a 224-unit condo tower stopped mid-floor, remains there today.

Asbury Park briefly came alive during Springsteen's visit to the city in 2002 to promote his new album *The Rising*, but even the most devoted Asbury fans are not sure if the city will rise again. "Young men on the corner like scattered leaves / The boarded-up windows, the empty streets," Springsteen sings in "My City of Ruins."

"Asbury Park's days as an entertainment center are over," Santana says, standing on the sidewalk outside the club. Levon Helm and David Johansen, among others, are playing this night. "It will be a bedroom community on the ocean, with shops and restaurants."

How does the Stone Pony fit into the picture? Santana is not sure. From the sound of it, he wants to get away from the club, get away from the debate, get away from the squabbling.

"I just want to go fishing, ride my bike, do things with my kids, enjoy the Shore."

Could he see selling the Stone Pony one day? "I hate that thought," he replies. "There are two voices going back and forth. My family is stronger right now, but that other voice is strong, too. Thank God I don't need a paycheck from this place. There are many nights you don't cut it, you just squeak by. There are nights I've lost $15,000 here."

Cookman Avenue, the main commercial drag, is showing signs of life. Sonny's, a heralded soul food restaurant, is often packed. Moonstruck, another popular restaurant, moved from Ocean Grove to Asbury Park. New homeowners, notably gays, are moving into and restoring the grand old houses.

How will it all turn out? No one knows.

"Asbury Park is an endangered American treasure," says Santana, who sees himself as part "of the band of pioneers who came here when no one else would come here."

Five Russian kids, tourists, saunter past, snapping pictures with a digital camera. Santana glances over, bemused. Most of the 65,000 hits the club's web site gets every week come from overseas.

"My other dream?" Santana asks. "I want to open a Stone Pony in Havana. Go back, fly the American flag, ride a Harley."

Miss Deckadance

"I have goose bumps on my tush!" Jillian Nuara yelps as she stands, in peach-colored Body Glove thong and matching minuscule top, behind a curtained-off area in Trump Marina.

"It's freezing in here," says Nuara, enrolled in the master's program at Stockton State College. "Can we turn up the heat for the half-naked women?"

Around her, beautiful young women—Nuara, at twenty-three, is the oldest—adjust their teeny-weeny bikinis and apply various lotions and gels, all the while checking themselves in a floor-length mirror. "Do you need baby oil?" one contestant asks. When her friend nods yes, she shouts, "Baby oil guy!"

The sole reporter behind the curtained-off area is not the baby oil guy, but, for the moment, wishes he were.

"Ladies," announces Kathy Walls, who is the only one, besides the reporter, whose attire doesn't consist of a piece of dental floss, "when you get on stage, walk back and forth. Work the stage. There will be no grinding. This is a classy pageant."

Nuara and ten other women pile into an elevator and head to the Deck, an outdoor bar at Trump

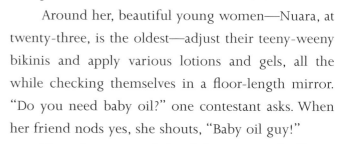

Kathy Walls, Hooters recruiter
and Miss Deckadance contest director

Marina. Aerosmith's "Walk This Way" blasts from speakers. The crowd erupts in cheers.

Another Friday night, another Miss Deckadance pageant.

The weekly bikini contest at Trump Marina would never be confused with, say, the swimsuit competition at the Miss America pageant. The smaller the suit, the better. Thongs? Fine, but Miss Deckadance draws the line at g-strings. No grinding, but who needs to?

"Atlantic City is home to the most dignified and glamorous beauty pageant in the world," says Trump Marina marketing vice president Todd Moyer. "This ain't it."

Most of the contestants at the summer-long competition are "Hooters girls," waitresses at the sports bar-restaurants of the same name in Atlantic City and elsewhere. But some contestants proudly note they are not Hooters girls and do not fit the restaurant ideal: a cheery, personable young woman who happens to be well endowed and look great in the trademark short, tight orange shorts.

"We're non-Hooters, non-boobs," says redheaded Debra Axelrod, an exotic dancer at a South Jersey club.

"I'm not a 10, not a 5," says Linda Bader, a corrections officer in Burlington County who intends to take the state trooper exam.

"I think you look hot," Axelrod tells her.

Bader harbors no illusions about what she is doing.

"There's no talent, no intelligence involved here," she explains. "It's how you look in a bikini."

Is she nervous? "Not nervous, not anything," she replies quickly. "Put on a bathing suit and walk onstage."

Linda Bader, a corrections officer

Bernadette DeSimone,
an aspiring singer

Angela Rafail, who won one of the weekly
Miss Deckadance contests

Contestants this night include blond-haired Bernadette DeSimone, an aspiring pop/hip-hop singer who gives an impromptu little concert, in her yellow bikini, on a terrace as she and her fellow contestants await the judges' decision; and the twin-sister bikini threat of Angela and Rebecca Rafail, whose car got a flat tire on the way from their home in Delaware. But they changed it, and made it to the pageant just in time.

And then there is Nuara, who undoubtedly is the only contestant who went from waitress at her local I-Hop to Hooters girl while working on her master's degree.

"Never worked out a day in my life," insists the five-foot-three Nuara. "Metabolism. I'm a pig. I'll eat anything you put in front of me. I don't exercise. I don't care."

Her mom's best friend gave her the nickname "Stickgirl," which she uses as an e-mail address. "I haven't weighed 100 pounds in my life," she claims. "It's all hair and boobs."

All Miss Deckadance contestants receive $50 for entering, plus a $25 food comp. First-place weekly winners receive $250, plus an automatic pass to the end-of-summer Miss Deckadance finals. The grand-prize winner receives a $5,000-value package of gifts, including $1,000 in cash.

"Why am I here?" asks Lauren Taylor, a nineteen-year-old from Ocean City. "There's money involved. You can win $250 for wearing the bathing suit you wear to the beach."

"I have four crowns," says DeSimone, one of three contestants from the Maple Shade Hooters. "Little Miss Gloucester County. Young Miss New Jersey. Young Miss Garden State. Miss Teen New Jersey. This is the first time I've done strictly bikini."

Angela Rafail would walk away with top honors tonight; the blond-haired, blue-eyed Hooters girl would join Nuara—the first week's winner—and thirteen other contestants the following Friday night for the big bikini showdown, the Miss Deckadance finals.

A dozen judges sit expectantly on stools in front of the stage, some with beer bottle–filled buckets at their feet. Girls will be judged on the basis of "stage presence," "physique," and "overall beauty," according to the judge's score sheet.

"Some girls do a circuit of bikini contests; they're everywhere, every weekend," says Walls, promotions manager and "recruiter" for eight area Hooters. Now thirty, she is a veteran of many bikini contests. "It's a great way to travel, a great way to make money. I've been to the Bahamas."

What does she look for in a prospective Hooters girl?

"A cheerleader type, the girl next door, the approachable beauty," she replies. "They have to have a great personality as well as a cute face."

The master of ceremonies is Mike Gill, who does afternoon drive for radio station WJSE in South Jersey. "They said, 'You're going to emcee a bikini contest all summer.' Uh, okay."

There is the usual adjusting of suits, spraying of tan amplifier, and spreading of baby oil backstage. Tara Thornton, a DJ and spokesmodel for WJSE, is, at twenty-nine, the oldest contestant in the finals. A former high school substitute teacher, she is wearing a barely-there plunging white bikini.

Jamie Haines,
a Hooters girl

"What it comes down to is personality," she says. "You can have a killer body and great suit and be dumber than a rock." She smiles. "You have to have the whole package."

Her fellow contestants seem to possess the whole package, and then some. Jamie Haines, a Hooters girl at Trump Marina, is an anesthesia technician at Cooper Hospital. Liesje Cardillo is a student at the University of Delaware, where she runs track.

Jessica Boughers, who works at a Hooters in Richmond, Virginia, is an Arena Football cheerleader. Miss Deckadance contestants filled out forms listing hobbies, dreams, and such. Boughers's philosophy on life: "You'll never get anywhere sitting on your butt." For the Miss Deckadance finals, she is going with the cowgirl look—rhinestone-studded black bikini and cowboy hat.

Stephanie Scalfaro, twenty-five, is a "knockout girl"—one of the women who hold up cards between rounds at casino fights—and has a degree in molecular biology/biochemistry. Shawna Bailey of Vineland is both Hooters girl and second-grade teacher. On the line for "measurements" on the form, she wrote: "No clue." Lesley Clarke's ambition: to be an FBI agent.

"Girls," Walls says before escorting her contestants onstage, "if anyone's looking for a job, come see me afterwards. You're pretty much a shoo-in."

So who would win the first-ever Miss Deckadance grand prize? Not the athletic Cardillo, in her star-spangled bikini, nor the slender, statuesque Scalfaro, nor curly-haired Jeana Morton, about to get her black belt in karate. It's the five-foot-four, 105-pound Thornton, the oldest contestant, who walks away with the $5,000 gift package.

Will there be more Miss Deckadance contests? "Absolutely," Walls replies enthusiastically.

Jessica Boughers
went with the cowgirl look.

Tara Thornton,
Miss Deckadance 2002

Well after everyone else has left the black-curtained dressing room, Miss Deckadance still can't believe she has won. Did she think she had a chance? "No!" Thornton replies. "What did I tell you? It all comes down to personality. I really thought Cowgirl was going to win."

She pulls out her cell phone and calls her dad, who gave her a dollar for good luck. She's going to hold on to that dollar for a while.

Lucky Leo

"You don't have to put this down," says Leo Whalen, feet up on his dining room table, his thirteen pairs of golf shoes—only part of his collection—on a rack around the corner.

The man known as Lucky Leo proceeds to describe his golf game, his real estate dealings over the years, his days as a teacher in Toms River, his first game of chance, going off on tangents with breathtaking ease.

"You don't have to put this down," he will say repeatedly in the course of a morning-long conversation, but, of course, you do, because whatever follows invariably is interesting. Leo Whalen—Lucky Leo—is one of those people seemingly incapable of a bad quote. Even his non sequiturs go somewhere.

"Why Lucky Leo?" he says of the name of his arcade and games-of-chance concession on the Seaside Heights boardwalk. "The two just went together. If my

Seaside Heights

170

What exactly is the red zone?

Seaside Heights

name were Harry, I could have called it Horrible Harry's."

For this Jersey Shore amusements tycoon, timing was everything. He bought his first boardwalk stand in 1955, a year after the Garden State Parkway opened. Business was good from the first spin of the wheel. Lucky Leo's wasn't cheaper than other wheels on the boardwalk—ten cents a play back then—but his wheels featured fewer numbers. Better odds meant more customers; Lucky Leo did so well his first summer he bought a car, a 1955 Mercury. Soon, he didn't even need his job as

Nighttime, Seaside Heights boardwalk

teacher at Central Regional High School. In 1961, Lucky Leo and his wife, Barbara, bought a home in Hollywood, Florida, and Leo started a career as real estate mogul, building apartments and condos in Hollywood and Hallandale and shopping plazas in Toms River.

The wheel of life had taken a favorable spin for Lucky Leo.

In 1975, he bought an entire boardwalk block—arcade, fifteen games of chance, and a miniature golf course—in Seaside Heights. "If you're not interested in crowds and commotion, this is not the right place for you," he told The [Seaside Heights] Review in 1974. As much as he liked action, he admitted even *he* needed to get away.

"You need a rest," he said. "That's why I don't think there will ever be any twelve-month operation here."

He was wrong on that point; Lucky Leo's—air-conditioned in the summer, heated in the winter—is now open year-round. His sons, Steve and Tom, run the operation; Lucky Leo's grandson, Jeff Weast, a Monmouth University student, is day manager. Lucky Leo spends his summers on the Jersey Shore, but come November he and Barbara are winging it to Florida, where he makes ample use of all those golf shoes, playing golf five times a week. He serves on the advisory board of a Toms River bank.

"Which doesn't mean anything," his wife cracks.

Boardwalk games have come a long way since 1955; CDs and DVDs have replaced dolls and Cannon bath towels, and Ma Ferguson's shooting gallery has since evolved into a paintball game called Shoot the Geek.

Now a spry seventy-five, Lucky Leo takes unending pleasure in talking about Seaside, the boardwalk, his golf game, and whatever else is on his mind, which seems perpetually on fast forward.

"I talk a lot, but then I get talked out," he confesses.

On the porch, he gives his visitor a bottle of wine someone had given him the night before. He is no longer involved in the day-to-day operation of Lucky Leo's, but he hovers around the business all summer, making sure the boardwalk empire he started in 1955 is running smoothly, like a well-maintained wheel.

"Not bad for a guy who damn near flunked out of high school," he says, smiling.

Middle of the Shore

On the good ship *Margaritaville*, the decor runs to plastic palm trees and parrot heads. Miss Liberty and Uncle Sam sing patriotically from a red-, white-, and blue–streamered boat, and Davy Crockett, muzzleloader in hand, an immense furry hat on his head, scouts the surroundings from the prow of his boat.

A group of merry twenty-somethings dance on the deck of their balloon-draped boat. Not sure who they are supposed be, except happy.

Hey, Rich Walsh, love your Mr. Peanut boat!

"It's Theodore the Tugboat, from the PBS series," Walsh says. "Every kid knows about Theodore the Tugboat."

Whoops. Blame it on poor visibility. It's raining, it's pouring, but the stormy weather scarcely deters Walsh and other participants in one of the Jersey Shore's more colorful events, the annual Bayman's Boat Parade at Tuckerton Seaport.

Think of it as a maritime Tournament of Roses parade: boat owners decorate their craft in the funniest, zaniest ways possible. The parade, held the end of August, begins and ends at the seaport, winding through Tuckerton Creek—that's Tuckerton "Crick" down here—past cheering, partying

Joel Mott, curator at Tuckerton Seaport and sometime Davy Crockett

Thomas the Tugboat. Bayman's Boat Parade,
Tuckerton Seaport

residents of lagoon-front homes. Dogs bark, American flags
wave, and kids beg boat owners to blast their horns. The
weather today is miserable, but thousands of people are
gathered on house decks, boat docks, and other vantage
points along the parade route.

A grinning, water-spouting whale is piloted by Fred
Watson of Atco and John Brossman of Mystic Island.

"It's glued, taped, tied, and Velcroed," Watson says of
the whale's gray fabric skin. Various sounds—crashing surf,
squawking seabirds—emanate from somewhere inside the boat. "Those are my
whale sounds," Watson explains.

The boatman's parade is one of many summertime events at Tuckerton Seaport, still largely a Jersey Shore secret. Vintage boats—skiffs, garveys, runabouts,
rowboats, and more—are on display at the Classic Boat Festival in August. The

Tribute to
9–11 firefighters

Front-row
seats

Miss Liberty,
all decked out

Ocean County Decoy and Gunning Show, which features hundreds of exhibits and vendors and the state duck-calling championship, is held in late September. A Fins and Feathers festival is held in June, a seafood festival in July. Also in July: the Green Head Fly Festival and Craft Show, with demonstrations in green head trap-box building, a children's fly-swatting contest, and a largest green-head fly competition. For dessert? What else—shoofly pie!

The seaport itself is reason enough to make the drive down Route 9. In a dozen re-created historic structures, you can learn about the trades unique to Barnegat Bay and its baymen: Hurley Conklin's Decor Shop. Parsons' Clam and Oyster House. Joe Dayton's Sawmill. The Skinner/Donnelly houseboat. The Marshelder Gun Club. All are staffed by seaport employees and volunteers, ready to explain and demonstrate their tools and crafts. At the Perrine Boatworks, you can take classes in sneakbox building; sneakboxes are tiny wooden boats used by duck hunters. You can even have your own sneakbox or garvey built, but there is a waiting list.

Classic boat,
Tuckerton Seaport

"Our mission deals with the maritime history of New Jersey, especially the baymen and their contributions," explains curator Joel Mott (who, incidentally, played Davy Crockett during the bayman's boat parade).

The seaport (*www.tuckertonseaport.org*) has come a long way since 1989, when John Gormley and a group of friends decided to build a hunting shanty where they could teach water fowling. Their vision widened—why not build a maritime Williamsburg? Financed by state and local funding and private donations, forty acres of land along Tuckerton Creek were acquired. About twenty more buildings, including a replica of the Hotel de Crab, which once stood in Harvey Cedars, are planned.

Whale of a job, guys. Bayman's Boat Parade

Charlie Schultz works at Perrine Boatworks, Tuckerton Seaport.

"Old hunters never die," reads a coffee cup inside the atmospheric hunters' lodge. "They just stay loaded."

Hungry? At Skeeters Seafood Cafe, you can feast on a Hotel de Crab Cake Sandwich, Tucker's Island Turkey Cobb Salad, and Clamtown chowder (Tuckerton was known, over the years, as Clamtown, Fishtown, and Middle of the Shore).

Inside the Tuckerton Yacht Club is a gift shop and the Jacques Cousteau National Estuarine Research Reserve Visitor Center. The 120,000-acre reserve, named in honor of Cousteau, the late naturalist, filmmaker, and author, is the focus of the "Life on the Edge" exhibit. Listen to frog croaks, learn about cranberries, and sit in a boat to watch a video of Rutgers University scientists in the field.

Inside a replica of Tucker's Island Lighthouse (the original crumbled into a raging sea in 1927), read about pirates and "mooncussers" (brigands who would lure ships onto shoals by flashing lights on dark, moonless nights), lighthouses, and the Francis Life-Car.

The U.S. Lifesaving Service started using the ten-foot-long corrugated metal boat as a lifesaving device after it successfully rescued 200 terrified passengers from the ship Ayrshire, which ran aground off Chadwick Beach in "a brutally cold blizzard" in 1850. By 1854, more than two thousand shipwreck victims had been rescued by the Life-Car.

Yes it is.

Posters extol the virtues of Sea Haven, a resort established on Long Beach Island in the late 1880s. "Superior to any other point on the coast," one poster boasts. "There are no land breezes, no mosquitoes, no malaria, no fogs and the pure saline atmosphere is a certain relief from hay fever and kindred ailments."

The best line you might hear at Tuckerton Seaport comes from Anne Bonny, who deserted her husband for the charms of the colorful British pirate Calico Jack Rackham. In 1720, Calico Jack and his crew were captured and brought to trial in Jamaica.

Anne's words to her lover, according to a display: "I am sorry to see you here, but if you had fought like a man, you need not have been hanged like a dog."

The Beach Cleaners

Dawn, Seaside Heights. The fellows have gathered at the borough public works garage on Grant Avenue, waiting for their boss, John Camera. Remarkably, they all look awake and ready to go. There's Miguel Aguilar, who has an uncanny gift for barking like a dog; Tom Springer ("He's my dad," he jokes about Jerry Springer. "I don't know why I'm doing this, I'm a millionaire!"); and Joe Crepezza, a beach cleaner for the past five years.

And then there's Rocky Celentano, who begins talking out in the parking lot, continues on his way inside, and doesn't stop until, well, he doesn't stop.

"I go out on the streets, pick up garbage and anything up that moves, even the ants and cockroaches," says Celentano, a Seaside Heights street cleaner for a dozen years. "I do the whole town by myself, street by street, ocean to the bay."

A sign on the bulletin board behind him reads: "Remember to call if you are not coming in or if you are going to be late. Lateness is not a virtue."

If Celentano and the rest of the gang are a few minutes late, it's understandable. In the summer,

Miguel Aguilar dumps out his basket.

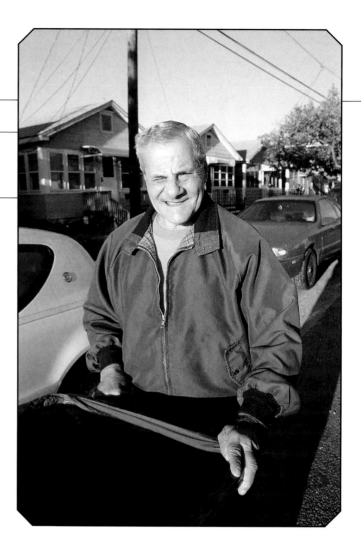

Rocky Celentano,
street cleaner extraordinaire

their day starts at four a.m. They generally work until noon. Celentano cleans the streets; Aguilar, Springer, and Crepezza clean the beach. Gifford Nevins's day begins even earlier. "Whitey" is out sweeping the sand clean with his beach rake at one in the morning.

In busy beach towns like Wildwood and Seaside, beach and boardwalk cleaners might pick several hundred cubic yards of trash daily in the summer. It's a never-ending accumulation of fast-food wrappers, cups, straws, newspapers, paper plates, tissue, cigarette butts, plastic forks and knives, takeout containers, cans, bottle caps, and cup lids. Those shorts someone left neatly hanging from a beam under the boardwalk? Leave them there; someone will take them. The couch? It'll find its way to its rightful home eventually.

The Seaside beach cleaners find jewelry, wallets, watches, and cell phones, which are deposited at the lost and found office on Hiering Avenue. And they find money—singles, fives, and tens, or, if they're lucky, a rubber-banded wad of bills. That they can keep.

"I found $104 the other week," Crepezza says. "Hundred-dollar bill and four singles. One beach cleaner found $500 one time this summer."

The tools of the beach cleaner's trade are not fancy—a "picker" to stab paper, cups, and the like, and peach baskets to put the garbage in.

"You can always tell how the town is doing by the garbage," one beach cleaner says. "If there's a lot of garbage, they're doing well."

One beach cleaner usually works the waterline; the others, the beach and under the boardwalk, then the boardwalk itself. They like to be off the beach by nine or so, when people start unfolding their beach chairs and spreading their blankets.

"Some people don't like the heat," says Angel Rivera, twenty-six. "But it's okay. I'm a big person, 240 pounds. I tend to sweat a lot. I get my hours in, get home before it gets really hot.

"Excuse me," he adds, stabbing a piece of paper on the boardwalk. "I have to keep moving."

Gary Bennett, another beach cleaner, is struck by the amount of clothes he finds. Not just T-shirts and bathing suits, but shorts, pants, and shirts. And shoes and sneakers.

"You wonder if they walked off the beach with any clothes on," he says.

The beach is cleaned several times a week in winter. "Then, it's mostly from the ocean," one beach cleaner explains. "Storms washing stuff up."

Whitey Nevins's day begins in the middle of the night.

Under the boardwalk. Beach cleaners, Seaside Heights

"I'm out there one, two a.m.," he says. The seventy-eight-year-old Lavallette resident has been Seaside Heights's beach raker the past two years; he was Lavallette's beach raker for nearly twenty years. He puts fifteen miles in every day, back and forth, back and forth, puttering along the beach in his John Deere tractor with attached Barber Surf-Rake.

He sets the rake about two inches deep, "so you don't pick up too much sand." How many teeth on the rake? "288," he replies quickly. How many laps does he do from one end of the beach to the other every morning? "About twenty-five," the former Navy cook says.

Some beach rakers will sift through the garbage when they're done for the morning. Not Whitey. He doesn't think it's worth the effort. But he did find $286— "it was rolled up in a rubber band"—on the beach the other day.

"It takes practice, lot of experience," he says of beach raking. "Some [rakers] don't go deep enough, or go too deep. All depends on the sand, whether it's wet or dry."

After he's finished raking, he hooks up a trailer for Beach 'n' Billboard, a Leonia-based firm that specializes in imprinting commercial messages in the sand. Beach 'n' Billboard's ads have appeared on beaches in Seaside, Beach Haven, Wildwood, South Padre Island, Texas, and Silver Beach, Michigan. For about twenty

Gifford Nevins, the beach rake operator for Seaside Heights

And this means you!
Sea Bright

thousand dollars, a company can get a half-mile of ads up and down the beach every day for a month. Each of the ads carries a "Please don't litter" tag line.

Back on the street, Celentano is picking up everything that moves and doesn't move. Twigs, cardboard, baby diapers, bugs. It all goes into his pan.

"This town wasn't clean before I got here," Rocky insists. "I should get a medal."

Old Barney

"I'm deathly afraid of heights!" Jackie M. of Oxford screams.

This is not necessarily a revelation one wants to have while perched on a narrow walkway sixteen stories above the rocks, but for Jackie the worst is over. She has just climbed 217 winding steps to the top of Old Barney for the most spectacular, panoramic—and vertigo-inducing—view along the Jersey Shore.

"We were going to go last year, but we had small difficulties with the car," Jackie explains.

Old Barney, of course, is Barnegat Light, whose slender red-and-white tower may be the most recognizable landmark on the Jersey Shore. Jackie is with her friend Nicole D. of Bethlehem, whose parents have a summer house on Long Beach Island. After some hesitation at the bottom and frequent let's-check-to-see-if-we-have-a-pulse stops on the way up, the two made it to the top, where what seems like the entire Jersey coastline unfolds in spectacular 360-degree BarneyVision.

"It's shaking!" Jackie suddenly says. "I feel a vibration!"

Long Beach
Island

Nice friend. Barney is not shaking, at least not today, although he does lean. Really.

In the summer of 2002, the U.S. Army Corps of Engineers discovered Old Barney had tilted twenty-one inches to the northwest in recent years. But not since January, when an earlier check had been done. The previous Barnegat Light, undermined by erosion, toppled into the sea in 1856. The forty-foot masonry tower, which marked a hazardous shoal as well as the 40th parallel, a point crucial to transatlantic navigation, had a "miserable" reputation as a lighthouse, according to the New Jersey Lighthouse Society web site (*www.njlhs.burlco.org*).

Old Barney, built one hundred yards farther inland, is not in any danger of falling into the sea. And standing on the open-air observation deck waaaaay above the ocean, you won't be able to detect any lean, to the northwest or otherwise.

"I thought it would be shaking; it's not shaking," says one visitor, peering below.

Stop it already!

Climbing Old Barney can be "very strenuous," according to a warning sign at the entrance.

We recommend you do not enter if you:

Have or had heart conditions

Have or had serious back trouble

Have or had recent surgery or illness

Are subject to dizziness

Are afraid of heights

It's a long way up.

Barnegat Light

The staircase is narrow, so if you're claustrophobic and afraid of heights, maybe you'd be better off choosing the teacup ride at the nearest amusement park for your thrill-seeking experience.

"It's nice up there," says Bruce Barrows, manning the front desk. "You can see the world."

You never know whom you're going to meet at Old Barney. Look who's here! It's Dorcas Preston, the reigning Ms. Senior America! She's on a whirlwind sightseeing tour led by Louise Ferla of Loch Arbor, vice president of Ms. Senior America Inc. Preston, of Corona Del Mar, California, is here for the Ms. New Jersey Senior Pageant at Trump Taj Mahal.

"I've been all over the country; no one's ever taken me to a lighthouse," Preston says.

Dorcas Preston, Ms. Senior America
at the time of this photo

Candy lover's dream, Long Beach Island

"I'm taking her around to show her there is more to the Garden State than Atlantic City," Ferla explains.

Old Barney, of course, is not the only lighthouse along the Jersey Shore. The yellow-and-black Absecon Lighthouse, on Pacific and Rhode Island avenues in Atlantic City, is the state's tallest light (see *www.abseconlighthouse.org*). It takes 228 steps to climb to the top; like Old Barney, it is open year round.

Cape May Lighthouse towers 157½ feet above the southernmost tip of the state. The Hereford Inlet Lighthouse in North Wildwood once was one of the more well-appointed along the Jersey Shore, with five fireplaces and beautiful quarters for the keeper and his family. Today, you can visit a small museum there and admire the lovely garden of flowers and herbs. The Twin Lights of Navesink tower 250 feet above Sandy Hook. And the octagonal-shaped Sandy Hook Lighthouse, at Fort Hancock, is the oldest operational lighthouse in the country.

But there's only one Old Barney. *The Star-Ledger* asked readers what picture or symbol should grace the tail side of 700 million quarters honoring New Jersey that the U.S. Treasury would issue in 1999. The readers' poll winner: Old Barney, edging out Thomas Edison and his light bulb, with George Washington crossing the Delaware, a legislative commission's eventual choice, a distant third.

"The most beautiful office in the world," Barrows says of his perch inside Old Barney.

And the magnificent structure—remember, it leans a little but doesn't shake—might be the best cheap thrill on the Jersey Shore. Costs you only a buck to climb to the top. Off-season, it's free.

Saving Flipper

Bob Schoelkopf has a lot of problems this morning, not the least of which is the woman and her supermarket lobsters.

A Lacey resident was so disturbed by the live lobsters at her local store that she bought all of them, took them home—and now wants to know what to do with them.

Schoelkopf is not usually into dinner-table marine mammal recovery, but he'll figure something out. After twenty-three years dealing with lost, stranded, injured, and dying seals, dolphins, whales, sea turtles, and other species, a few healthy supermarket lobsters should pose little challenge.

"This is the gray seal pup that's going to the Detroit Zoo," Schoelkopf, director of the Marine Mammal Stranding Center in Brigantine, says of one of his newer arrivals. The seal washed ashore in Harvey Cedars. "It had a fractured jaw. Infection set in. Without teeth, he cannot catch fish."

A more recent case: a seal that had been "peppered" with gunshot and blinded in one eye. Brought to the center from Virginia, the seal was given a regimen of antibiotics. After a few days in the pool out back, it was released.

The center, located across Brigantine Boulevard from Special Pizza City, rescues and rehabilitates stranded and otherwise stressed marine mammals and sea turtles. Staffers receive thousands of calls a year. Most are legitimate, but many people apparently don't see the "marine" part in front of the words "stranding center."

"We get bird calls—'I have a duck, I have a bird with broken wings,'" Schoelkopf says. "We've had calls for river otter. Possums. Lizards on people's front lawns. African monitor lizards. Turtles hit by cars or trucks, squashed turtles, turtles deader than a doornail. We can't do anything about those."

One caller reported a "big alligator" in Spring Lake. Schoelkopf's response: "We don't have equipment to handle alligators."

Every once in a while, a bizarre-sounding call does turn out to be legit.

Bob Schoelkopf, director of the Marine Mammal Stranding Center, Brigantine

"Guy calls in the middle of the night—'There's a penguin walking down the middle of the street,'" he recalls. "I said something like, 'Put it where the sun don't shine.' The next day I read in the paper where a rare rockhopper penguin was found up north."

The recovery work started in 1976 when Schoelkopf, then running a marine show—"Captain Bob and His Dolphins"—on Steel Pier in Atlantic City, received a call from city police about a whale that had washed ashore in front of Convention Hall. Schoelkopf spent two hours in the water trying to keep the whale wet, then had it towed to a nearby Coast Guard station. The whale was given IVs but died five days later. The necropsy revealed the whale had died simply of old age.

"It was my first lesson that not everything is salvageable," Schoelkopf says. "It's part of a natural process. If an animal's on the beach, it's probably already 90 percent gone."

A year after handling the Atlantic City whale, Schoelkopf and his wife, Sheila Dean, were running the first nonprofit, full-time, paid-staff stranding center in the world, in Gardner's Basin. "A one-room shed with a saltbox roof," the former navy corpsman not-so-affectionately recalls. "At that time we were looking at seven animals a year. This year alone we've done eighty-three seals already. Big change."

He and his network of six hundred volunteers statewide have since retrieved more than two thousand animals: Harbor porpoises, the smallest marine mammals native to the East Coast, entangled in fishing line. Turtles with plastic bags wrapped around their flippers. Dolphins scarred by boat propellers. Loggerhead turtles with gunshot wounds or harpoons embedded in the bodies. Whales struck by freighters.

"These freighters are so huge they don't even know they've hit the whales most of the time," Schoelkopf says.

Not all the stories have sad endings. A right whale spotted in the Delaware River turned out to be an eleven-month-old named Shackleton that had wandered all the way from Bay of Fundy. Shackleton eventually returned home.

The stranding center has made a name for itself beyond the rescue and rehabilitation of marine mammals. It was the first to recognize and report to the federal government the onset of the great dolphin die-off in 1987, when seven hundred dead dolphins washed ashore along the East Coast after being stricken with a deadly virus. The center also developed a specialized harness for moving large whales and a surgical technique for stabilizing fractured sea turtle shells with steel pins.

"[The National Aquarium in] Baltimore came up here to see our seals," Schoelkopf says. "We've developed feeding techniques for seals that are quite innovative." A center in Hawaii, rife with stranded dolphins, asked if he could provide special stretchers for wounded animals. Five were made, and shipped out.

The center, which attracts fifty thousand visitors a year, includes an administrative building and laboratory, a gift shop/museum, and various rehab tanks and pools. The center hosts dolphin watch cruises and various fundraisers, including a Swim for the Dolphins and a Harbor Seal 5K Run/Walk (for more information, go to www.mmsc.org). One of the newer and most popular programs is a week-long dolphin excursion and swim in the Bahamas.

The city charges the center one dollar annual rent, but Schoelkopf feels it's only a matter of time before Brigantine sells the valuable boulevard property to a developer. The lease runs out in 2009.

"It's gotten to the point where Brigantine says, if you want to buy this property, you can have it for a million and a half," says Schoelkopf. He shrugs. "If we don't reach some kind of agreement, we're out of here."

Where, he doesn't know. By his estimate, the center has done work in 126 communities around the state, but only 2 have donated any money. The center, with a $350,000 annual budget, depends largely on donations and gift shop sales. There is the occasional bequest, like the nuclear physicist from Cape May who willed the center $40,000. "Never met him," Schoelkopf says of the donor, who apparently once saw him administer to a stricken seal.

A poster in the gift shop spells out first aid for stranded mammals:

Notify stranding center
Keep the animal calm and quiet
Keep the skin wet
Keep clear of the blowhole, mouth, and tail
Keep everyone back

The last is particularly important; who doesn't want to see a creature from the depths up close? But "cuddly" animals can be dangerous. Seals, in particular, have dagger-sharp teeth and can inflict life-threatening bites because of the host of bacteria in their mouths.

Besides the everyday problems and challenges, Schoelkopf and the center face an uncertain future.

"Every year there seems to be more and more [regulations] to deal with," he says. "The federal government is now asking us to put a vet on call twenty-four hours a day. That could cost us up to $100,000 a year."

Just the other day, the company that insures his truck, equipped with a 1,000-pound lift, informed Schoelkopf it was canceling the insurance because the center was "too close to the water."

"It's kind of hard to run a marine mammal stranding center and not be near the water," Schoelkopf says.

Big Mike

Big Mike Henry, a crucifix around his neck and a Betty Boop screensaver on his computer, spreads his considerable girth in his chair and announces that his Rambo-style days are over.

At age forty-seven, the owner of Big Mike's E-Z Bail Bonds in Atlantic City—a former Navy Seal, stuntman, bounty hunter, and bodyguard—is just getting too old for this stuff. No more kicking down doors, chasing bail jumpers down the street, or staring down various and sundry weapons.

"I've been shot at, and chased by a guy with a bazooka," he says. "But the [worst] one was a grandmother who came after me with a tree axe. I was supposed to pick up her granddaughter for a court date. Grandma comes to the door and very sweetly says, 'I'll go get her.' She closes the door and returns with the axe. She

Better behave, or Big Mike will get you!

Can't beat that.
Atlantic City

chases me for two blocks with the axe like she wants to chop off my legs. My partner pulls over in the car and I jump through the window."

Guys with bazookas and axe-wielding grandmas—no wonder Big Mike, bail bondsman, doesn't want to get physical any more.

"My favorite stunt now," he says, smiling, "is to try to get a key to the place. I don't want to be Rambo anymore."

It doesn't mean Mike Henry is getting soft; it just means he's altering his business approach.

"There is only one Big Mike," says a flyer. "So do not let the other bail bondsmen fool you."

He was forced to put out the word when some local bail bondsmen started calling themselves "Big Mike," even though their names weren't Mike and they weren't very big. Imitation may be the sincerest form of flattery, but there's room for only one Big Mike in Atlantic City.

Uh, what kind of danger?
Atlantic City

And don't forget "Cash for gold."
Atlantic City

"I was never going to be a doctor, I was never going to be a lawyer," Big Mike says of his career path. "I did what work I could find."

He spent one year at Atlantic City High School ("I wasn't one of the best students in the world"), dropping out to work a succession of jobs, from bouncer/doorman at a local bar to sandwich maker at a Margate sub shop. In 1972, his parents moved to California. A neighbor built cars for stunt work, and got Mike a job as a stuntman in movies and TV. One stunt, in Palos Verdes, involved his hanging onto a rope ladder suspended from a helicopter. The rope broke, and Mike fell thirty feet to the ground, rolling another seventy.

"Broke my shoulder, my hip, both my legs, right arm, dislocated my jaw," he recalls. "By the time they got me to the hospital, I was a mess."

He cleaned pools, repaired bikes, owned several nightclubs. In between stunt jobs, he worked as a bounty hunter. On his first job, a fugitive jumped from a window, landing on Mike. They wrestled on the ground before Mike subdued him. Mike acquired a new nickname: "the drop-in bounty hunter."

"I'm not a rough man," insists Big Mike, who is six-foot-three, 390 pounds. "I was always known as the pussycat bounty hunter."

"He could put the fear of God into you just by his voice," his ex-wife Marge—the two remain good buddies—says.

A pack of Marlboros lies unopened on the desk. "You can call us collect from jail," reads a flier on the wall. "We have the key to freedom. We will get you home."

Big Mike will send you back to jail if you cheat on him. "Con man of the year" is how Big Mike describes one recent client, who broke into his father's house and stole five hundred dollars to make bail.

Once, as a bounty hunter, he found his man hiding in a dryer. "I turned it on. You heard this 'ca-boink, ca-boink.' I said, 'Anybody hear anything? Is that coming from upstairs maybe?' The kid screams, 'Help, I'm in the dryer!' "

Another time, a kid he was chasing took one look at Big Mike and said, "Oh, shit, the Titanic's after me!"

In Florida, he picked up a guy wanted on drug and weapons charges and drove him back to New Jersey, promising him if he behaved himself Big Mike would take him to a go-go bar on the way home. At a strip club in North Carolina, Big Mike gave the kid ten dollars in singles, but kept the handcuffs on.

"Business can be very boring," he says. "You're on stakeouts. A lot of guys end up looking like me. We like our 7-Eleven sandwiches."

One of Big Mike's mobile office vans

Fashion statement.
Atlantic City

When he moved back to New Jersey six years ago, he ran a plumbing business for a year, then got into bail bonds. "Being a bounty hunter is more about being slick," he explains. "Being in bail bonds is more about judging a person when they walk through the door."

Big Mike works out of a storefront on Atlantic Avenue. The previous tenant: a fortuneteller. He operates three mobile vans, enabling his staffers to process bonds at jails or the family's home. He doesn't have high opinions of some of his competition. "The most crookedest outfit on earth," he says of one. "Crooked one minute and straight the next," he says of another.

You have to judge not only who walks through the door, but also who's already inside. One employee stole $18,000 from him last year. Mike takes credit cards and checks, but many people just stop in and make their payments in cash. The money is often put in a drawer. The money sometimes goes missing.

"Lot of cash in this business," Big Mike says. "You get sticky fingers. Two things you learn in this business—get it into the safe or get it into the bank."

His backbreaking/door kicking days as a bounty hunter are over. But the hours are long. Today is Labor Day; he's in the office. "I take two days off a year. My birthday was yesterday, which I did not take off."

The bondsman's dream: to buy two small hotels, one in Atlantic City, one in Fort Myers, and use them as his retirement fund. For the time being, though, he'll remain Big Mike. There's only one; accept no imitations.

"It's a rough business, and it's a darn good business," he says. "You have to be a little crazy."

To those even thinking about skipping out on bail, he makes the same promise: "When I tell you I will come for you, I will find you. I will not hurt you, but I will bring you back."

Grassy Sound

Ed Hainsworth clambers from under his house on stilts, looking like he just went ten rounds with a lady mud wrestler. His face is streaked with grease and goop; black splotches stain his T-shirt, shorts, legs, and sneakers. He is replacing pilings, an essential duty in the town he lives.

"This is the way we live down here," the retired state trooper says as he settles into a chair.

"Here" is Grassy Sound, the town that time and the rest of New Jersey forgot. The Garden State is home to 566 municipalities that include scores more hamlets and villages, but none is more determinedly isolated than Grassy Sound, population, at any given time, about fifty. It is just minutes from the Wildwoods, and technically part of Middle Township, Cape May County, but might as well be in a world its own.

The state's most determinedly isolated community, Grassy Sound

Ed Hainsworth,
president,
Grassy Sound
Civic Association

Forty-five homes—a few no more than weather-beaten shacks—arch across an expanse of marsh and muck. A narrow boardwalk leads from one home to another and from the homes to the road, a quarter-mile away. In a storm, the boardwalk becomes impassable, cutting off the inhabitants from the outside world.

The residents of Grassy Sound wouldn't have it any other way.

"People who come down here," says Grassy Sounder George Frame, "have always wanted to be left alone."

"This is the seashore without the traffic, without the noise," Hainsworth adds.

They don't realize it, but hundreds of thousands of Wildwood-bound vacationers drive by Grassy Sound every summer; it lies along Route 147, which connects the Garden State Parkway to North Wildwood. But few have visited Grassy Sound, even though it is an easy detour off Ocean Drive.

If you live at Frame's end of town, you can't park your car anywhere near your house. You leave it by the side of Ocean Drive and walk hundreds of yards along the boardwalk, which zigzags across the marsh.

Grassy Sound is not the literal end of the road in New Jersey; Cape May is ten miles south. But no other community in New Jersey is as removed from the world of strip malls and suburban sprawl.

"The people who live here are a little like hermits," Frame explains.

"The hole in the wall gang" is what his wife, Lory, calls her fellow Grassy Sounders.

The gang includes the Frames, wildlife consultants and writers; Florence Love, who lives in what is believed to be Grassy Sound's former brothel; and Hainsworth, who, like George Frame, spent summers here as a kid. Other Grassy

Be it ever so humble, there's no place like home.

End of the boardwalk, Grassy Sound

Sounders include a doctor, a furniture store owner, a retired bar owner, and a semi-retired steeplejack.

"Interesting characters, pioneer-type spirits fighting the elements all these years," former Grassy Sounder Michael Laird once said of those who have called Grassy Sound home. "It's like living on the Midwest prairie."

Laird bought his house for $2,400. "It was nothing more than a closet up on broomsticks that pigeons lived in," he recalled fondly.

Today, houses in Grassy Sound go for as low as $20,000—but good luck buying one. Property here changes hands as infrequently as season tickets to the Green Bay Packers. When a house is sold, it often goes to a member of the family. Dozen of empty lots are scattered across the mile-long marsh, but state wetlands regulations forbid building on them. Hainsworth owns the newest house in Grassy Sound; it was built in 1964. The result is that Grassy Sound looks much as it did thirty, fifty, even one hundred years ago.

Forty years ago, the owner of the local general store would load up his red wagon and make the long journey down the boardwalk, dropping off supplies at each house. Today, many Grassy Sounders bring in food and supplies on their own wagons, walking hundreds of yards along the boardwalk to their front doors.

"I feel like a bag lady, pushing my things in front of me," Frame says, smiling. "But it's fun."

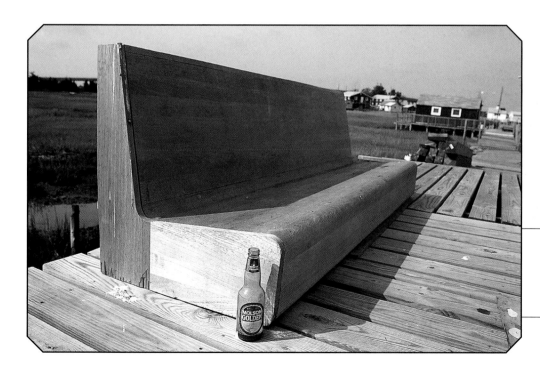

Contemplation corner, Grassy Sound

Shackside advertising,

Grassy Sound

In the early 1940s, his parents bought a prefab shack, brought it down by truck, and set it along Ocean Drive. The owner of the property told Frame's parents they couldn't put the house there, but if they wanted, he could sell them one.

Hainsworth's mother, his Aunt Sophie, Aunt Stella, grandmother, and various other relatives—fifteen in all—would visit every summer, jamming into his Uncle Walt's house.

Uncle Walt—Walt Kendzierski—still lives in Grassy Sound. At eighty-two, not only is he the town's oldest resident, but he's also lived here the longest.

"We hated coming down here," Hainsworth says, laughing.

But he and his wife rented a house here in the 1980s. When the house next door came up for sale, they bought it, for $20,000. He figures he's put another $30–$40,000 into it since.

"I was crabbing all the time," Frame recalls of his childhood summers in Grassy Sound. "We went fishing in the creek. It was a good habitat for eels . . . sea spiders [spider crabs]. Now the sand bar has built up quite a lot, so there isn't much fishing from the houses anymore."

Fishing isn't what draws people to Grassy Sound these days. It is the panorama of water and sky, the natural beauty, the splendid isolation, and the marsh. Wildwood is minutes away; it might as well be hours.

Many Grassy Sounders live here summers only; the Frames are among a dozen or so people who live in Grassy Sound year-round. Winters here make cabin fever seem the least of your worries. The wind howls constantly, rattling windowpanes. A severe storm can flood the boardwalk, cutting off access. The silence and solitude are almost unsettling. The homes, fortunately, are cable-ready.

"And yes, we have telephones," Hainsworth says.

In the 1880s, the Anglesea Land Company envisioned Grassy Sound as a shore resort. The company started selling lots and built the Anglesea Railroad, which connected Grassy Sound to nearby Burleigh. An 1882 map shows hundreds of lots spread over the marsh—where there are about forty homes today.

Anglesea Land Company's plans never took hold. By 1884, there was little more than a hotel, several dozen cottages, and a boardwalk.

There is not much more today. Until recently, Grassy Sound's future seemed tenuous. In 1992, the state ordered Grassy Sounders to stop dumping sewage into the surrounding wetlands or risk losing their homes. About half of the homes found in violation were condemned and demolished, easing the way for the construction of a new bridge over Grassy Sound.

The state's de facto message to the remaining residents was simple: Build a sewer line or move out. The Grassy Sound Civic Association, incorporated in 1991, built the line, with its own and federal and state funds. Today, just about everyone in Grassy Sound is hooked up. It wasn't cheap; the line initially cost homeowners $13,000 each. They also pay a $300 quarterly sewer fee, and a $50 monthly fee to the civic association. Isolation has a price.

The town has applied for listing on the New Jersey Register of Historic Places.

"Anything we can do to preserve the future of Grassy Sound we have tried and will keep trying," says Hainsworth, president of the civic association and an investigator for the Gloucester County Board of Elections. "In New England, the historical value of a Grassy Sound would be recognized. We're not some Johnny-come-latelys who suddenly popped up here on pilings."

To Frame, Grassy Sound doesn't have quite the same appeal it once did. Lights have been added on the Ocean Drive toll bridge near his house. When the wind is blowing a certain way, he can hear conversation from the "tap rooms" in North Wildwood.

But he allows "it's nice being in the marsh."

"There's a saying here," says Hainsworth, about to do battle with his pilings again. "Once you get the mud between your toes, you'll never leave."

Sunday Morning at the White House

Nadine Caporilli's Sunday morning goes like this: Mass at Saint Michael's Church in Atlantic City, then a cheesesteak with lettuce, tomato, and fried onions at the White House Sub Shop, two blocks away.

"A heart attack waiting to happen," laughs the Galloway resident, sitting at the counter of the fluorescent-lit sub shop at the corner of Arctic and Mississippi.

In other words, cheesesteak—and hoagie—heaven.

"I'd rather eat in a place like this than a stuffy restaurant serving foo-foo sandwiches," she says.

Nadine Caporilli, a White House regular

No foo-foo food at this White House; there is no better sub shop at the Jersey Shore. Other places offer bigger subs. Other places offer a wider range of ingredients. But none can match the White House's combination of fresh meat and ultra-fresh rolls, delivered a half dozen times daily by a bakery around the corner.

The help is charmingly gruff, the atmosphere borderline chaotic. Take a ticket and resign yourself to what is usually a long wait. Soak up the surroundings— the assembly-line sandwich production, photos of celebrity customers (everyone from Joe DiMaggio to Tiny Tim), neon signs. Nine booths, five stools. Tastykakes in a display rack. Managers Phil La Rocca and

The Beatles ate here.
White House Subs

Tony Arcodia, a high school principal, is one
of the sandwich makers at White House Subs.

his brother Tommy, with a combined ninety years served at this White House, can
be found behind the counter. Phil talks, Tommy doesn't. All the sandwich makers
may seem businesslike if not brusque, but they're funny, personable guys if you get
to know them. Even Tommy's funny.

Tony Basile, fresh out of the service, opened the White House Sub Shop in
1946. Tony's still around. The Beatles, Frank Sinatra, Bob Hope, Donnie and Marie
Osmond, the last few Miss Americas—they've all been here. On the wall is the
towel Sinatra used in his last Atlantic City appearance, in July 1991.

And you still want to go to your local sub shop?

How thoughtful. Aaron Colelli spread a towel before placing his sub on a friend's Mercedes.

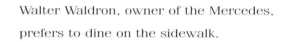

Walter Waldron, owner of the Mercedes, prefers to dine on the sidewalk.

"I've come here since 1969," says Margie Morgan, one regular. "I came up from Georgia, didn't even know what a sub was."

She has mailed White House subs to friends in Atlanta, Seattle, even Germany.

No designer subs here. And you don't have to dig through a mountain of lettuce, tomatoes, and onions to find a few scraggly pieces of week-old meat. This is what you can get at the White House: ham, cappacola, salami, and provolone, in various combinations. Cheesesteaks, meatball, and hot sausage sandwiches, and a "fancy white" tuna fish sub. That's it.

The meat is neatly folded around slices of cheese and thinly chopped lettuce and topped, if you wish, with hot peppers. Each sandwich is wrapped in orange butcher's paper and then a double layer of nuclear war–proof wax paper. It won't seep grease on the front seat of your car.

In 1946, a whole sub cost 50 cents. Today, a whole sub costs about $10.50. A half sub is big enough for one.

Terrie Merendino has been a White House waitress twenty-six years. The sandwich makers include Tony Arcodia, the principal of Avon Elementary School in Barrington. Tony's been at the White House thirty-four years. Tony Basile is his uncle.

"We are not affiliated with any other sub shop in this area or any other area in the world," reads a sign in the window.

It is not known whether John, Paul, Ringo, and George went with the Regular White House sub or the White House Special sub when they were here.

As Caporilli finishes her cheesesteak inside, Aaron Colelli, Walter Waldron, and Jay Bergstrom are outside, eating their subs on the sidewalk. Colelli's sub sits on Waldron's Mercedes. Colelli, thoughtfully, spread out a towel on the hood before chowing down. The three, bleary-eyed, spent the previous night at Colelli's bachelor party at Caesar's. He's getting married next week.

"You can call this the last supper," the groom-to-be says, laughing.

World Series of Surf Fishing

Tom Sylvester rumbles down the beach in a borrowed Jeep Cherokee, his tires fishtailing in the soft, deep sand. For a good two miles, the beach is packed with fishermen and fishing poles, lined up in neat little rows.

"One in the cooler!" a fisherman suddenly yells.

"I'll get you a judge," Sylvester yells back.

It is not an invitation to help yourself to a beer; it means there's a fish in the cooler, and it needs to be measured.

Nearby, Jim Jefferys stands, rod in hand, eyes anxiously sweeping the water.

"Got a croaker and a kingfish," he says, disappointed. "Tough pickings today."

The World Series of Surf Fishing is under way, and the pickings will have as much to do with luck as with talent.

"We're using bloodworms, bunker, mackerel, and clams as bait," says Walter Harris of Southampton.

"Clams were the trick today," reports John Martorano of Cherry Hill. "Everything was hitting clams."

Love the shades.
World Series of Surf Fishing

Ted Kinter of Brant Beach and his
31 ½-inch striped bass

The two belong to Tom Snyder's Fishing Club, named after one of their members. Next year, Harris would like to change the team's name to "The Deep Six" or something colorful. Pay the fifty-dollar entry fee to the World Series of Surf Fishing, you can call your four- or six-member team anything you want.

The tournament, in its fifty-sixth year, is run by the Long Beach Island Fishing Club, headquartered in the old Coast Guard station in Harvey Cedars. The competition, held several weeks after Labor Day, attracts two hundred surf fishermen from New Jersey, Pennsylvania, Maryland, and elsewhere.

Walt Llewellyn,
member of the
Brigantine
Sharks team

"I think I've got a [striped] bass!" Sol Weinstein of Pennsauken shouts. He winds his reel feverishly, the line screeching, and drags his catch ashore.

"Bass my ass," he says disgustedly. A sea robin is twitching at the end of his line.

Some teams are surf fishing–circuit regulars; others are husband-and-wife teams or guys who rounded up a couple buddies from work. Most drive down for the day; several dozen sleep in bunk beds and cots on the fishing club's second floor. Members gain access year-round by coded cards; they can relax in a cozy lounge with mounted striped bass, sailfish, and dolphin on the walls and 1950s-vintage Naugahyde sofas.

Bob Burstein is tournament director; Sylvester, a Philadelphia fireman, is beach master, riding up and down the beach collecting scoring forms from his judges. The fishermen share the beach, this morning, with surfers, a few of whom don't exactly welcome the anglers' presence. "F——g fishermen," one twenty-something surfer says loudly as Sylvester's Cherokee rolls by (although another surfer does apologize repeatedly later to a fisherman for getting tangled up in his line).

Jefferys, from Horsham, Pennsylvania, has competed in the World Series of Surf Fishing since 1976; he is president of the Association of Surf Angling Clubs (*www.asaconline.org*), which sanctions this and other tournaments.

Walt Llewellyn, of Bensalem, Pennsylvania, a past president of ASAC, is a member of the Brigantine Sharks, composed of his wife, Wendy, and parents, Walt and Jo.

"Been on this island forty years," the younger Llewellyn says. "Spent summers in Surf City."

Eighty percent of the fishing he does is surf fishing. "It's peaceful. You're sitting on the beach relaxing. You don't have to worry about another boat. But you have to be more patient. You pick a spot, maybe two spots for the day. It's not like you can move around."

"To me, it's a one-on-one battle," his dad explains. "You're in your environment, the fish is in his."

The Surf 'n' Land team is serious about surf fishing; they have two teams for competitions. They've also won the World Series of Surf Fishing the past ten years.

"There are no secrets," Weinstein says. "We use fresh bait, live bait when we can. Most of us can cast farther than the rest of these guys—400, 500 yards."

In fact, one team member, Gary Borne, once held the world record for casting.

"I don't like boat fishing," Weinstein says. "Tried it once. Me and another fellow chartered the boat. Caught 187 bluefish. Too much like work, too monotonous. Out here, it's no fish finders, no depth finders, just you and the fish."

At noon, the tournament's end, the fishermen pull up their poles, pack up their trucks, and drive over to the club. A lunch buffet is set up on the deck. The Long Beach Island Fishing Club takes surf fishing—and eating—seriously; three separate crews cook the food for various club events. Picnic tables are spread out in the warm September sun. Plaques and prizes—rods, reels, tackle boxes, boat buckles, Chesapeake Bay atlases—fill several tables. Long Beach Island Fishing Club members are not allowed to enter the World Series of Surf Fishing, but there would be other tournaments to enter, other opportunities to fish.

"You're more independent [than other fishermen]," Burstein says. "You go when you want to go. You don't have to drag a boat around. You know what they say about boat owners, don't you? Your two happiest days are the day you buy your boat and the day you sell your boat."

Send in the Clowns

Being a clown can get expensive, and that's not funny. Check out Bonky G Bird's outfit. Translucent blue braided hair—$65. Frilly pantaloons? Another $65. Shoes—$75. Red-and-white wool socks—$5 apiece. And the wooden-stick smiley face Bonky G Bird uses as a prop? That costs only $1.99, thank goodness.

"It adds up," Bonnie Bohadel says. "I clowned for four years before I got my first pair of shoes."

The Seaside Heights boardwalk is crawling with clowns, and all they want to do is make you laugh. Clownfest, the largest and longest-running clown convention in the country, is under way. More than three hundred clowns take over Seaside an entire weekend in late September, weaving up and down the boardwalk in high-wheeled bicycles, juggling balls, doing pratfalls, and bringing smiles to the faces of young and old.

"Hey there, want to pet my squirrel?" Bill Tedeski of Pittsburgh asks a five-year-old girl. The green-haired, red-striped-suited clown is holding a wiggling, furry—and fake—creature that he describes as "a North American legless."

A purple-haired clown wears a white straw hat dotted with butterflies. A 400-pound clown—Little John, of course—zigzags across the boardwalk on a little scooter that surely will not be able to bear his considerable weight. "Eat a prune. Start a movement," reads one clown's pin. "God made clowns just for fun," says another.

Tedeski's been a clown since he was nine. Hubba Bubba, otherwise known as Mike Eremus, started clowning six years ago. His wife took him to Clownfest as a birthday present. While many clowns go on the clown circuit, hiring themselves out for birthday parties and promotional appearances, Hubba Bubba's a "nonprofit clown." He donates all fees to charitable groups and organizations.

"I've been a Bubba all my life," he explains. "I added the Hubba."

The Maccungie, Pennsylvania, resident is an EMT. "Don't tell anyone this is what I do for fun," he says.

Hundreds of clowns prowl the Seaside boardwalk during Clownfest.

Eremus, like any clown, first had to figure out what kind of clown he wanted to be. A "whiteface" clown is elegant, quiet, reserved. A character clown is a cop, fireman, doctor, or nurse, for example. An Auguste clown uses slapstick. Eremus, a juvenile probation officer and volunteer fireman, originally intended to be a hobo or tramp, but figured he was "too comic," so he became an Auguste. Laughs are him.

Hubba Bubba is a part-time clown, but you can do this full-time. Dean Martin does. The former Boeing employee and Wichita resident now goes by the clown name of "Crunchy."

"Anyone who's willing to share their heart can be a clown," Martin says. He became a clown on April Fools Day, 1989. Working for Boeing at the time, he was going through some admittedly "weird" times personally. Clowning provided a release. "It's a great place to hide," Martin says.

What do you call a really big clown? Little John, of course.

These guys
and gals know
how to have fun.

Dean Martin, a k a Crunchy, of Wichita, Kansas

He quit his job in 1994 to clown full-time. Crunchy—a nickname his brother gave him when they were young, Martin is not sure why—does everything from carnivals to cruises; he appears in costume in Mary-Kate and Ashley Olsen's "Birthday Party" video.

How much does Crunchy charge? In Wichita, where he lives, his bookings start around $100 an hour. "I've heard of clowns in Dallas charging $150 an hour for that birthday party. I've heard of clowns in New York City charging $200 for that birthday party. When people hear that, they say, 'What?' What they don't see is the forty-five minutes to an hour it takes to put on your makeup. The time it takes to drive back and forth. Your balloons and upkeep."

What do his three kids from his first marriage think about his new calling?

"They like the dad but they think Dad's a lot happier when he's a clown," says Martin, forty-eight.

The clowns get down to business during Clownfest; there are sixty classes in magic, makeup, juggling, and other topics.

"For a lot of clowns, this is a recharge of the batteries," says Marilyn Caruso, a clown from Staten Island who has attended all twenty-one years of Clownfest. "I'm going to go home, clown my heart out."

"I don't have any stickers left, but can I have a hug?" Bonky G Bird asks a little girl on the boardwalk. "The G stands for gorgeous. I can't help it."

She started out as a whiteface. "Very prissy, very quiet—that's not me," she explains. Once, a clown by the name of Cousin Otto walked up to her and asked, "What are you doing?" Her reply: "I'm clowning." "Are you a porcelain doll?" he asked sarcastically. She decided then and there to become an Auguste. She loves making kids smile, but her favorite audience is senior citizens. "Nobody loves them, nobody gives them a hug," she says.

Sometimes a kid will not want to be hugged, or even entertained, and a clown needs to recognize that. "A good clown always respects other people's space," according to Martin.

And what if you're having a bad day in the real world? How do you transform from unhappy human to happy clown?

"Sometimes it's tough," Martin replies. "But when you put on that nose and happy face, your character takes over. When you see that first kid's smile, all your troubles fade away."

Acknowledgments

"What a job!" friends jealously remarked when I told them about this book. "You get to spend all summer at the Shore. That's not work!"

Maybe so, but this "dream" assignment would have been impossible to pull off if not for the cooperation of scores of people up and down the coast.

To Matt Applegate, Mike Barchi, and the rest of the crew at Aerial Sign, for letting me spend two days at the banner sign operation.

To Bob Ruffolo, director of the New Jersey Fresh Seafood Festival, for the golf-cart tour of the festival grounds.

To Karen Bence and Mary Ann Izzi at Jersey Shore Haven, for showing me around the Airstream-only campground.

To Sgt. Harry Vliet, assistant station commander of the New Jersey State Police marine unit's Point Pleasant station, for his professionalism and patience, and for the ride across Barnegat Bay.

To Jon Stevenson, director of the Boardwalk Chapel, for the story of his unusual seaside ministry.

To Steve Murphy, a k a Tiki Murph, for the memorable midsummer afternoon underneath one of his tiki bars. I promise to replenish the beer supply next time I stop by.

To Domenic Santana, owner of the Stone Pony, and Phil and Tommy La Rocca, managers of the White House Sub Shop, for the lowdown on these two Jersey Shore landmarks.

To Kathy Walls, Hooters recruiter and Miss Deckadance contest director, for backstage access at the bikini contest.

To Jean Webster, the dynamo who makes Sister Jean's Kitchen go, for taking time from her never-ending mission of feeding the down-and-out.

To Mark Soifer, the genius behind Weird Contest Week; and to Jack Morey, executive vice president of the Morey Organization, for his take on wacky, wonderful Wildwood.

To the staff of the Ocean City Baby Parade, the Jersey Shore's single most colorful spectacle.

To Bob Burstein, Tom Sylvester, and other members of the Long Beach Island Fishing Club, for a front-row seat at the World Series of Surf Fishing.

To Lacey Nicholl and Tara Whalen, for letting me take their pictures at Tee Time in Ocean City, and all the people who patiently waited while this amateur photographer fiddled and fretted with film, lenses, and light.

To David Shotwell, administrative officer of the Ocean Grove Camp Meeting Association, for giving me the grand tour, and Richard and Ruth LeDuc, for graciously allowing me inside their tent.

To Tim Ferrante, publisher of *Game Room* magazine, for putting up with me on all those miniature golf courses. Keep working on your game!

To John Camera, head of the Seaside Heights public works department, for letting me make the rounds with his beach cleaners; and Leo Whalen, a k a Lucky Leo, for the history of his Seaside arcade operation.

To Bob Schoelkopf, director of the Marine Mammal Stranding Center, for taking time from his around-the-clock job; and Ed Hainsworth and the rest of the residents of Grassy Sound.

To Mike Henry—Big Mike—owner of Big Mike's E-Z Bail Bonds, one of the more unforgettable characters I met in the course of the summer.

To Mike and Miriam Kohr, owners of the legendary boardwalk custard stands; and to Marvin Hume, the "mayor" of Sunset Beach, for the story behind the nightly flag-lowering ceremony.

To Pete Dunne, director of the Cape May Bird Observatory, for letting this non-birder tag along on one of his Monday morning walks.

A big thanks to Christine McCabe and the rest of the lifeguards competing in the All-Women Lifeguard Tournament at Sandy Hook. OK, I admit it— that morning did not qualify as work!

To Celia Maybaum, Hot Dog Queen of the Jersey Shore; and to Jim Merritt, Kate Cook, Tony Raniero, and Brian Vernachio, for making the weekend on Sedge Island an unforgettable one.

To colleagues at *The* (Newark, N.J.) *Star-Ledger*, for their encouragement and support.

Thanks to Kathie and Bert at Freese Camera in Highland Park, for once again making me look good.

And where would I have been without Bob and Anthony and all the guys in the service department at Seaview Jeep on Route 35 in Ocean Township? They kept my trusty Jeep running beyond the 500,000-mile mark (the Sahara has since gone to that great Jeep junkyard in the sky).

To my mom, Connie Genovese, my "agent" and biggest booster, still going strong at eighty.

Saving the best for last, I can't say enough about all the friendly folks at Rutgers
   University Press for making this book possible. To Director Marlie Wasserman,
   for once again saying yes. To Marilyn Campbell, who has played such a
   key role in all four books I've done for the Press. To Ellen C. Dawson, for
   the terrific interior design and layout, to Trudi Gershenov, who created
   the colorful, eye-popping jacket, and to Anne Hegeman for production
   coordination. I can't forget the people in the warehouse—Janet Tamburrino,
   Carmen Rodriguez, and Max Rodriguez. And anything but a Bronx cheer for
   diehard Yankee fan Lisa Gillard Hanson, best publicist in this or any other
   galaxy.

To all those who opened their doors or made room on the sand for me during
   the summer of 2002, many thanks. I hope I have done your stories, and the
   one-and-only Jersey Shore, justice.

Bloomsbury, New Jersey
April 2003

About the Author

PETER GENOVESE is a feature writer for *The* (Newark, N.J.) *Star-Ledger*, for which he also does the summer-long Munchmobile series and a weekly "Eat with Pete" column. He is author of *Roadside New Jersey*, *Jersey Diners*, and *The Great American Road Trip: US 1, Maine to Florida*, all published by Rutgers University Press, and *New Jersey Curiosities*, from Globe Pequot Press. He has appeared on CNN, the History Channel, the Food Network, and elsewhere, and was among the "40 New Jerseyans We Love" in the January 2003 issue of *New Jersey Monthly*. A native of Trenton, Genovese lives in Hunterdon County.

9-11 Memorial, Ocean City